S0-ARV-983

WENDAMEEN

The Life of an American Schooner from 1912 to the Present

Captain Neal Parker

Down East Books
Camden, Maine

Photo by Ed Glaser

Thank you to Amory Carhart and Marion Marsh, grandchildren of Chester W. Bliss; to Robert Brumder, nephew of Robert and Erwin Uihlein; to Paul L'Amoreaux and Paul L'Amoreaux Jr., the son and grandson of Paul L'Amoreaux; to Paul Pfeiffer and his wife, Frieda; to Richard Coburn, Doug Hall, Major Chadwick, Captain Edward Glaser, Reuel Parker, and many supportive friends for their generous help in keeping the *Wendameen* alive. Also, thank you to Susan Milisa Mustapich for her countless hours of assistance with research, writing, editing, and support.

Unless otherwise marked, the photographs in this book are from the collection of the author. They represent only a portion of the documentation available for the *Wendameen*. Anyone having or wanting further information about the schooner should contact Captain Parker at 207-594-1751 or www.schooneryacht.com

ISBN 0-89272-582-6

Library of Congress Control Number 2001012345
Interior and cover design by Lindy Gifford

Printed by Versa Press, East Peoria, Illinois

5   4   3   2   1

DOWN EAST BOOKS
P.O. Box 679
Camden, Maine 04843

For orders and catalog information, call 800-685-7962,
or visit www.downeastbooks.com

To the memory of Professor Carl Beam, who once told me, "Whatever you do, do deliberately."

Professor Carl Beam and I aboard the skipjack *Mamie A. Mister* in 1983.

Wendameen?

During my years of research, I have come across about half a dozen old accounts defining the name *Wendameen*. Most are similar.

The general consensus holds that the word is Delaware Indian for "large catch of fish" or "successful fisherman." One early newspaper account states that "wendameen" is Norwegian, with a definition similar to the above. Several Norwegians whom I spoke with had never heard the word. I have gone through books on American Indian cultures and inquired of local tribal leaders, but I still found no clue, though I am convinced the word is rooted in a Native American language. Many yachts at the time of the *Wendameen*'s launching bore Indian names. It was a way for the "new Americans" to pay tribute to a fast-disappearing culture.

A notion came to me while working with a local carver to recreate the scrollwork on the bow of the *Wendameen*. Early photographs revealed that the gilded design was most unusual. It began with a forward-facing crescent moon. It reminded me of the shark fins that used to be nailed to the bowsprits and jib booms of large sailing ships for good luck. Of course, coastal tribes would have respected the shark as the greatest fisherman of all. Also, the *Wendameen*'s design is rooted in the greatest fishing vessels of her time, the Gloucester schooners.

I have satisfied myself for now, at least, that "wendameen" could well be a native word for shark.

Introduction

We were to leeward of the fleet at the start of Maine's 1990 Schooner Race. The *Wendameen* was on her shakedown cruise following an extensive restoration. She had not sailed in fifty-seven years.

The wind was light sou'west as I tried to work the 67' vessel up to a fleet of twenty-two other schooners. A dark line on the horizon showed that a better breeze was fast approaching. Finally it hit us, fresh from the south and steady. A racing log entry from 1924 came to life: "The Wendy bows to the breeze like she's tickled to death with it, and off we go like a train of express cars!" She overhauled one schooner after another. Many were twice her size. As she flew by, there came cheers from the other vessels, for their crews had heard the *Wendameen*'s story from their captains. By the end of the race, she had danced by most of the fleet, all good boats with skilled captains.

That race became the exclamation point marking the end of a four-year restoration that most said could not be done.

Launched in 1912, the *Wendameen* was the first schooner designed by the brilliant yet then undiscovered John Alden of Boston. I first saw her when I was a teenager; it was 1974 and she was stored in a shed on City Island, New York. The old girl had not sailed since 1933, but I remember how cigar smoke and perfume still filled her saloon and how the sounds of music and laughter still seemed to resonate throughout.

I grew up, moved to Maine, sailed schooners, and became a captain. A dozen years went by before I found myself again standing on what was left of the *Wendameen*. She was dying on a mud bank in Connecticut.

Most of her deck had collapsed from rot, and much of her topside planking had fallen away. She had neither rudder nor engine. Only memories held together her fifty-six tons of wood, bronze, and iron.

The ghosts were still aboard. I could hear the rush of feet on the schooner's foredeck as she came about, and I smiled as curses wafted out of the engine-room hatch. I saw the teeth of a fine wave under her bow as she reeled off the knots. I stared at her, and she looked back.

I bought the *Wendameen* in the fall of 1986. Hiring a small fishing dragger, I tried to tow her to Maine, but after ninety miles, a strong easterly forced us to seek refuge in the Thames River. Just a hundred yards from a New London dock, the dragger lost steering. Wind and tide conspired, and set the *Wendameen* against the pier. I secured her lines, and a small voice said, "Wait 'til spring." Shortly afterward, I discovered that the *Wendameen* had taken herself someplace familiar. She was berthed less than half a mile from her original mooring and her first owners' home. This was to be one of many coincidences that eventually tied the schooner's new life to her past.

It was two years before I raised enough money to install an engine and rudder, which finally brought the *Wendameen* to Maine. I lived on rice and frozen pizza, drove a car with no brakes, and heard hundreds of people say, "Give it up." But a few believed in me and the *Wendameen*. Much support came from descendants of the schooner's early owners. She had played such an important role in the lives of those she touched that even generations later, grandchildren and nephews still knew her story.

I hauled the *Wendameen* at Rockland in the fall of 1988, just down the coast from the yard where she was launched decades before. I worked alone through the winter, replacing most of her frames. Finally, a bank showed mercy, and I was able to hire a shipwright.

On July 1, 1990, we cast off and set the *Wendameen*'s 2,400 square feet of sail. The reborn schooner was underway! A guest pointed to a forgotten news clipping in the scrapbook. Carrying the date July 1, 1912, it read, "The new auxiliary schooner yacht *Wendameen* went into commission this morning, her owner and party aboard. . . ."

That night, long after the guests had gone to sleep, I sat on deck alone. I thought I saw a couple of guys playing poker in the cockpit, and every once in a while they looked up at me and grinned.

The cockpit, 1922.

Foreword

by Reuel Parker

In 1981 I took a summer job as shipwright at the South Street Seaport Museum in Manhattan. While working there, I met a restaurant owner who was deep in the throes of a major sailboat restoration on nearby City Island.

Tony felt he was losing ground—that the boat was deteriorating faster than he could rebuild her—and sought my professional opinion. He had been at it for seven years, and although he was a very talented carpenter, he didn't have experience in major boat restorations, and he didn't have a plan. But Tony was in love with the boat, and as soon as I saw her, I understood why. She was a 1927 John Alden-designed Malabar Junior—a shapely 29' wineglass-transomed hull with a radically tall 54' mast. Her workboat heritage was obvious, but equally evident was the evolutionary process that John Alden had applied to the type. Even in her advanced state of decay, she looked as if she could fly.

John Alden is one of my idols. His designs, often generated from New England fishing vessels, are to my eye as beautiful, pragmatic, and high-performance as boats can possibly be. Of course there are newer designs that are faster and more weatherly, but "performance" in the highest sense of the word must include seaworthiness, seakindliness, safety, comfort, and durability. As fast as an Open 60, a maxi-racer, or a big catamaran may be, none of them is as beautiful or as comfortable to sail as an Alden.

I took on the Malabar Junior project, and when she was finished and we sailed her, the experience was like living poetry. Heeled sharply, close-hauled to weather under full sail in twenty knots of wind, *Imagine* laid her lee rail right to the edge of the water in such a perfect curve that the sea slid along her side exactly parallel to the rail cap and released her cleanly at the transom. She sailed the way a fish swims, the way a bird flies. She outpointed and outpaced a 30' go-fast fiberglass sloop one memorable day on Long Island Sound. The sailors on that plastic-and-aluminum caricature of a boat were bundled in layers of foul-weather gear and looked soaked to the skin. Those of us on *Imagine* were dressed in street clothes and were as dry as if taking a stroll on Seventh Avenue. I will never forget the looks on the other crew's faces as we passed them.

While working on *Imagine* on City Island, I had met a wonderful old man named Gerry Ford. He was a retired naval architect with an amazing collection of derelict yachts. Though in his eighties, he had every intention of restoring and sailing all of them. One was the early Alden schooner *Wendameen*. Mr. Ford took me all through her, and I felt the same way Neal Parker felt when he discovered her. It was love at first sight.

Seven years later, in the summer of 1988, I met Neal on the waterfront in Camden, Maine. We became friends almost instantly, finding that we had many interests in common. He took me out to see the *Wendameen*, barely afloat in the outer harbor. She was very far gone, but Neal was full of enthusiasm. We entered the hull through a hole in her side. The decks were completely rotted away, covered in places with scraps of plywood. If you set foot in the wrong place, anywhere on board, you went through. The Camden "city fathers," led by an apoplectic harbormaster, were doing their level best to tar and feather Captain Parker and ride him out of town under the keel of his hideous eyesore of a derelict sullying their precious postcard-perfect harbor.

Neal was a major topic of conversation in Camden. The polite opinions labeled him an impractical dreamer. The rude opinions are not worth repeating. Virtually everyone said his project couldn't succeed. They didn't know Neal. I was skeptical but supportive. I knew the restoration could be done, and I knew it was a monster of a job. Through brilliant planning, dogged perseverance, self-imposed poverty, and unbelievable economy, Neal made the *Wendameen* sail again and did it in record time, for less money than even I thought possible. I am proud to have helped.

In 1990, the *Wendameen* took on her first passengers, mere hours after I had frantically rolled paint on her decks. Fortunately we had started aft, where they came on board, and the paint there was almost dry. We cast off our dock lines and motored into Rockland's outer harbor. When *Wendameen*'s sails went up and she came alive, the experience was like my first sail on *Imagine* but on a much grander scale. I can still feel that thrill. Now, in 2001, after sailing as Neal's guest every summer over this past decade, I must state that there is really no other experience on Earth quite like sailing on the *Wendameen*.

Reuel Parker is a marine architect, a shipwright, and the author of books and magazine articles on boat design, construction, restoration, and history.

John G. Alden
An architect is born

Young naval architect John Alden turned up his collar as he stood in the bows of the fishing schooner *Fame*. The January wind shrieked through his wet oilskins, sending shivers through his tired limbs. He watched a government steam cutter come alongside, ready to pass a towline to the almost wrecked *Fame*. Anchored well off the New Jersey coast, the schooner had for a day and a half tried to attract attention from any vessel that could offer assistance. Now, after a ten-day ordeal at sea, Alden would be glad to see the safety of New York Harbor. In his frozen daze he thought back to the warmth of his office and drafting table, where the whole adventure had begun.

Alden was hunched over a ship's draft in early December 1907, at the Boston office of yacht designer B. B. Crowninshield, when Crowninshield announced that his fishing schooner *Fame* was stranded in Halifax, Nova Scotia. The 120' vessel was stuck there because her captain and twenty-three crewmen had been quarantined ashore after a smallpox outbreak on board. Alden, with his love

John Alden, in shirtsleeves, supervises the last stages of construction aboard the *Wendameen* at the East Boothbay yard of Frank Adams. The carpenter at right is installing the steering gear.

Winter gales battered this unidentified Gloucester schooner. She is covered with tons of ice, which might have sent less able vessels to a watery grave.

of adventure and sailing, volunteered to put a relief crew together and bring the schooner home. He knew Crowninshield was concerned that the boat was losing money each day she was not out fishing. What he did not know was that the crew had been forced ashore against their will.

Alden, who was twenty-three at the time, found four other volunteers. Three had some sailing experience, but all were younger than he. Crowninshield sent an experienced captain ahead to see that the *Fame* was fumigated. When Alden and his crew reported to the vessel in Halifax, the young designer quickly realized that the skipper was old, tired, and without interest in anything beyond the warmth of the woodstove in his cabin and his master's pay. Alden could have called it quits then, but instead he took charge.

He was unprepared for the hostile reception from the other fishermen in the port. They resented the young upstarts who were taking away the schooner and jobs from the *Fame*'s real crew. This thwarted Alden's plans for finding experienced hands to help sail the schooner back to Boston, but not wishing to disappoint Crowninshield, he and his small crew prepared to get the boat underway themselves.

Unknown to Alden, the Fame's quarantined captain was conspiring to have the vessel seized. He confessed to authorities that he had purchased bait without a license, in violation of Canadian law. This breach gave officials the power to seize the schooner. Now just one step ahead of the law, Alden and his jury-rigged crew were forced to slip their anchor in the middle of the night and head out into the ice and storms of the North Atlantic.

On the first day, they encountered a blizzard that forced the schooner into the Gulf Stream. Alden and the crew managed to put a reef in the main just before the jib "split into atoms," in Alden's words. The winds increased, and with seas washing aboard and all holding on for dear life, the mainsail started to tear. All hands managed to furl what was left of the *Fame*'s four thousand square feet of sail. Much to Alden's delight, the schooner responded handily with just her foresail and staysail.

Despite this small victory, Alden and the *Fame* were not about to get a break. For days the crew was wet and frozen. Ice formed on deck and in the rigging, weighing the schooner down and making her stagger with each big sea. But every time, the *Fame* managed to shake off the tons of seawater and keep going. By the third day the crew started to run out of food and drinking water, as they had been unable to get supplies in Halifax. And the gale that tossed the big schooner about continued to drive her from her destination.

That the short-handed vessel survived in this weather was remarkable to Alden. When he and his companions finally saw land, they were off the southern coast of New Jersey. Though the wind continued to ravage the *Fame,* the exhausted crew, now confident of their position, worked her inshore. With the barest tatters of sail set, the schooner was able to hold the desired course. The wind was blowing sixty miles an hour, and the air temperature was well below freezing.

Using their only remaining anchor, and with their hearts in their throats, the crew of the *Fame* made a desperate attempt to drop the hook. Down went the six hundred pounds of iron and eighteen hundred feet of line. The anchor burrowed into the sandy bottom, and the *Fame* was brought to, her head to the wind. Alden thought, "We survived." The final leg of the adventure was at hand. As the rescue cutter approached, a blast from its deep horn brought Alden from his daze as he caught the towline. Soon he would be comfortably ashore.

John Alden was greatly impressed by his experience aboard the *Fame,* which managed to survive in spite of the weather and the inexperienced crew on board. Back in the comfort of Crowninshield's office, he was determined to base his career as a naval architect on bringing the qualities of the Gloucester fishing schooners to his designs.

In 1909, Alden opened his own office on the Boston waterfront. His first commissions were small boats. These established his reputation for designing fast and sturdy craft that could endure anything the sea had to offer. As Alden's reputation grew, so did the size of the vessels he was hired to design. He must have recalled his experiences aboard the *Fame* when he was commissioned to design No. 21, his first big schooner yacht, a project initiated in 1911 for Elmer J.

Standing amidships, John Alden talks with a shipwright as the yard crew varnishes the mast hoops and completes the rigging. Note the canvas loosely wrapped around the bow line to keep it from chafing the newly varnished rail.

Alden's Design No. 21, the 67' schooner yacht *Wendameen,* from an original newspaper photo.

Bliss of Boston. When Bliss commissioned the vessel, he may have been thinking of replacing his 65' schooner, the *Venona.* However, for reasons unknown, before the keel was even laid, Elmer passed the project to his relation, Colonel Chester W. Bliss, of Springfield, Massachusetts.

Design No. 21 would become the *Wendameen.* When Alden developed the new 67' schooner, he drew her relatively narrow with a sweeping sheer and long ends that would allow her to meet and ride each oncoming wave. Her construction was to be massive, more like a workboat than a lightly built yacht. But there her similarity to a workboat ended.

The *Wendameen* was to be finished in varnished mahogany, white trim paint, and nickel-plated bronze fixtures. The owner had a large stateroom with a private head. There were accommodations for three guests and a cabin for the three crew members. The large saloon with its tufted velvet cushions and electric lights was ideal for entertaining. If the wind gave out, the auxiliary engine would keep the vessel moving at a full twelve knots.

This new schooner was one of the designs that launched Alden's career as a pioneer of comfortable cruising yachts that were also suitable for ocean and long-distance racing. Within ten years, his boats would dominate the American scene. He preferred to have his designs built in Maine shipyards. By using shipwrights accustomed to building sturdy vessels at prices fishermen could afford, he placed his boats within the means of the newly emerging middle class. Alden must have inspired confidence because his wealthy clients could have had their yachts designed by anyone.

The yard selected to build design No. 21 was the Frank Adams Shipyard in East Boothbay, where it produced everything from large and small steamers to fishing schooners and cargo carriers.

Chester Bliss
The good life

The *Wendameen* was launched in the spring of 1912. Her owner, Chester W. Bliss, was president of the Boston and Albany Railroad, like his father and grandfather before him. The B&A was the most lucrative rail line in New England on a per-mile basis, and its success rivaled that of the Vanderbilts' New York Central. The Bliss family's involvement in railroads dated back to the early 1800s, when the B&A was one of the first in the country. Thanks to its success, Chester Bliss inherited a fortune at a time when the average American family could live on $400 to $500 a year.

In addition to heading the railroad, Bliss was president of the Chapin National Bank in Springfield. As such, he was prominent in the community, but mostly he was a gentleman of leisure. Though Colonel Bliss called Springfield his home, he enjoyed summers at his other residence in New London, Connecticut. His small mansion at 979 Pequoit Avenue was considered to be a showplace of the summer colony.

The Bliss family was at the center of the New London social scene. A member of the prestigious New York Yacht Club, Chester owned several boats over the years. He was a founder of the Pequoit Casino Club, a small Victorian palace that was a recreation spot for the wealthy. Bliss and his wife, Isadora, hosted many well-attended parties at this seaside watering hole, as well as in their home.

New London was also a summer retreat for the Bohemian set—the artists,

Col. Chester W. Bliss enjoys life aboard his schooner during a summer cruise in 1913.

The Pequoit Casino Club 13

actors, and writers who were escaping from New York City's sweltering streets. Bliss often enjoyed the company of Eugene O'Neill and Katherine Anne Porter, among others in the New York literary scene. The *Wendameen* was moored within sight of the house on Pequoit Avenue, and on easy afternoons, the Bliss family and its guests cooled off aboard the schooner in the gentle summer breezes of Long Island Sound.

Chester Bliss's comings and goings were often reported in the society pages and yachting news of the *New London Day,* the *Boston Globe,* and the *New York Herald,* among others. The *Wendameen*'s first appearance in her home-port was announced in the June 24, 1912, edition of the *Day*:

"Colonel C. W. Bliss's new schooner yacht arrived Saturday. She is in command of Captain Frederick W. Grimpe of this city and came from Boothbay, Maine, where she was built. . . . The new yacht was the object of admiration of the other skippers in port."

Nor was the vessel ignored by nautical publications. According to a September 1912 review in *Yachting* magazine, "The *Wendameen*'s construction is probably heavier than any other yacht of this size . . . yet she sails well in anything but a calm . . . and can carry whole sail when everything else is seeking shelter."

Though Bliss already owned a motor yacht, his attentions quickly turned to his new schooner. As was typical of the small yachts of the day, a full crew was not kept on board; Captain Grimpe, however, was employed throughout the year.

The rest of the paid crew consisted of a cook and engineer. One of the cooks was usually borrowed from the summer house, and Bliss's chauffeur, after carrying the bags aboard, changed hats and doubled as ship's engineer. Once underway, Bliss and his guests would join in the sport of sailing; hoisting sail was a job for all hands. Bliss started what was to become a longstanding

Spanking new, the *Wendameen* motors out for the photo shoot on which her commissioning painting would be based.

This is the first photograph of the *Wendameen* under sail. There are several pencil lines filling in some missing rigging detail.

Chester's wife, Isadora.

Bliss had a lively reputation. At a fancy costume ball where his wife, Isadora, dressed as European nobility, hostess Minnie Butt dressed as Mistress Mary Quite Contrary. According to the September 1, 1913, *New London Day,* the men made up enough sailors "to man the convict ship *Success.*" Bliss, breaking with the more traditional costumes, appeared in Vaudevillian blackface. At another social event he showed up in a dress, having squeezed his big 6'4" frame into a petticoat.

A guest known only as Eleanor. Behind her at the helm is Captain Fred A. Grimpe.

Katherine Anne Porter in 1913. In a few years she would begin her writing career and become one of America's leading novelists.

The wind is light and the *Wendameen* sports a big Yankee jib, fisherman staysail, and main tops'l. This photo, taken prior to 1915, was used by the brokerage firm of Gielow and Orr.

The Wendameen in 1914 as she sails into the sunset for Chester W. Bliss.

tradition by placing a gramophone on deck. Music filled the air and was a constant source of entertainment.

Newspaper clippings from the period tell of Bliss's world through weekly accounts on the *Wendameen*. The schooner was constantly busy:

The *New York Herald,* July 1, 1912: "The new auxiliary yacht *Wendameen,* Mr. Chester W. Bliss, N.Y.Y.C., went into commission this morning, her owner and party aboard, taking a trip to Montauk."

The *New York Herald,* July 19, 1912: "The auxiliary schooner yacht *Wendameen* . . . has returned from a week's cruise to the eastward with her owner and son, Addison, on board."

The *New London Day,* September 30, 1913: "Auxiliary schooner yacht *Wendameen* was hauled out at Riverside today and launched after one blade of her broken propeller wheel had been cut off to balance the wheel."

The *New London Day,* November 5, 1913: "Schooner yacht *Wendameen* will not go out of commission right away, contrary to previous reports. The yacht will be used several weeks longer by Colonel Chester W. Bliss in hunting on Fishers Island."

Bliss had three children. The oldest, Elizabeth, was married; the youngest, Isadora, was fourteen. The middle child was a son, Addison, who Bliss hoped would carry on the family legacy. Addison was twenty years old and studying at Harvard University when the *Wendameen* was launched. He often accompanied his father on board during hunting and sport-fishing expeditions along remote parts of the New England coast. Sharing hunting, fishing, sailing, gin, cards, and cigars, father and son became very close.

When Addison graduated from Harvard in 1914 and started his own life, Bliss put the *Wendameen* up for sale. Without his son to accompany him, he spent less time on the schooner. During the summer of 1915, he chartered her to the Wanamaker Flying Expedition. The *Wendameen* was scheduled to sail to Newfoundland to meet her clients. At the last moment, however, the flying expedition was cancelled. Instead, the charter party cruised the coast of Maine for the month of July.

Before the summer ended, the three-year-old schooner was sold.

In January 1917, twenty-six-year-old Addison took a steamer to France as a volunteer with the U.S. Ambulance Field Corps, just four months before the United States declared war on Germany. Chester Bliss would never see his son and sailing partner again. During the ten-day voyage, Addison contracted pneumonia, which was common aboard the crowded ships, and he died February 22 at the American Hospital in Neuilly, France. From that point forward, his father slowly withdrew from the society life he had enjoyed so much.

In 1925, Chester W. Bliss and his wife decided to make the house in New London their year-round residence. It was a place of fond memories. After an extensive remodeling of the house on Pequoit Avenue, they moved in. During his first night home, at the age of sixty-five, Bliss died in his sleep. Perhaps his last thoughts were of Addison and the *Wendameen*.

The very dapper Addison Bliss aboard his father's motor yacht, *Raccoon*, in the summer of 1915. A note on the photo suggests the family was aboard to watch the Harvard-Yale crew races, which were held on the Thames River in New London.

Robert and Erwin Uihlein
The Milwaukee years

Erwin Uihlein. Shot glass at his feet and pipe at the ready.

Chester W. Bliss sold the *Wendameen* in 1915 for about $10,000. The transaction was handled through Gielow & Orr, one of the foremost yacht brokerages of the time. With the sale, the schooner journeyed from one of New England's leading families to one of Milwaukee's powerful brew masters, the Uihleins. Thus began the *Wendameen*'s career on the Great Lakes.

The passage to Milwaukee started with a trip to New York City and up the Hudson River. At Troy, just above Albany, the *Wendameen* entered the Erie Barge Canal. Her masts were removed so she could pass under the numerous low bridges. Sails would not be needed in this narrow, winding waterway. The canal, which opened in 1825, was primarily a commercial route used to transport grain and produce from farms in the Midwest to markets in New York.

The *Wendameen* motored through both rural countryside and industrial centers on the 360-mile westward journey to Lake Erie. She crossed the wakes of steam tugs, cargo barges, and the last few mule-drawn barges, remnants of an even earlier time. The yacht must have seemed out of place alongside this hardworking company. Once she arrived at Buffalo, on the edge of Lake Erie, the masts were restepped, and the *Wendameen* sailed for the remainder of the trip north, through Lake Huron and into Lake Michigan to her new homeport, Milwaukee, Wisconsin.

Robert and Erwin Uihlein (pronounced "Ee-line") were the *Wendameen*'s new owners. They were sons of Schlitz brewery president August Uihlein. Eventually, the brothers would run the brewery, along with the family's other ventures. Erwin, 31, the younger of the two, was a skilled sailor and navigator. He and Robert often made extended trips on the Great Lakes with close friends. During the summer of 1916, one cruise involved their going to Lake Superior for two weeks of hunting and fishing with a paid Native American guide. Great Lakes merchant sailor Jimmy Ellington, "Old Jimmy," served as professional seaman and would remain with the *Wendameen* until 1933. Photographs of the trip reveal a hardy crew made up of the Uihleins; their first cousins, the Pabsts; and their friends the Schaffers. Bill Brumder, Robert and Erwin's nephew, was also on board, as he was for many of the *Wendameen*'s cruises. Seventy-two years later his younger brother, Robert, would provide the seed money that helped save the *Wendameen* and assure her restoration.

The brewery families of Milwaukee, though competitors, were on friendly terms. As the temperance movement gathered steam, they had to work together to present a united front. When Wisconsin went dry in 1916, the brewery families began a battle to win back public opinion. To combat Prohibition—and the women's suffrage movement that supported prohibitionist candidates—the Schlitz and Anheuser-Bush breweries invested $36,000 in a publicity campaign. That venture placed favorable beer and brewery stories on the front pages of eleven thousand newspapers nationwide.

Nonetheless, events continued to turn against the brewers. The American war effort was competing with them for grain to feed the troops. The brewers, who were mostly of German descent, further hurt their cause when they attempted to assist the most powerful journalist of the time, Arthur Brisbane, in purchasing the *Washington Times*. They were trying to save their industry by attempting to turn public opinion against Prohibition, but it was a bad time for powerful German families to align themselves with a newspaperman whose editorials were known to be for sale. In Wisconsin, the Anti-Saloon League condemned "Schlitzville-on-the-Lake" and "Kaiser brew." Prohibitionists argued that German brewers were contributing to industrial disorder at a time when efficiency was essential for national survival. In Washington, the Senate ordered an investigation into the allegedly disloyal behavior of the brewers. In October 1918, President Wilson signed a bill prohibiting the manufacture of intoxicating beverages.

In spite of accusations and strong anti-German sentiment, the Uihlein brothers did their duty. Erwin served the war years in the U.S. Navy, and Robert was on the executive committee of the Milwaukee Council of Defense. By May, the *Wendameen* was again listed for sale with Gielow & Orr. With the country at war, the brothers had little time for yachting.

The schooner's new homeport would not be far away. For the next decade, she would hail from Chicago, and her life would grow even more colorful.

While the *Wendameen* raced through the roaring '20s with a new owner, the fortunes of the Uihleins took a few more twists and turns, and eventually improved. When the Depression began in 1929, the brothers renewed their alliance with editor Brisbane in an effort to oust President Hoover, a staunch supporter of Prohibition. The group raised $300,000 to support the candidacy of Franklin D. Roosevelt, known to be sympathetic to the brewers' cause.

After his landslide victory in 1932, Congress permitted production of 3.2 percent beer, or "near beer." Erwin Uihlein, who had wisely kept the brewery equipment in working condition, helped put the family back in business. Four years later, Prohibition was repealed. In 1933, and for the next three decades, Erwin served as president of Schlitz. Robert became vice president and director.

After losing the Prohibition battle, in 1919, the Uihleins fought back using their entrepreneurial spirit. Speculating that the public might turn from beer to sweets, they developed a product line bearing an anglicized version of their name. The "Eline" Milwaukee Old Style Chocolate and Cocoa Company was born. The family's new chocolate factory was an extravagant showplace. The lobby was paved with Italian travertine marble, and every office had a fireplace. No expense was spared in production or marketing. But the Eline Old Style Chocolate and Cocoa Company ceased operation in 1928, after its almond bar started appearing without nuts, its gumdrops were so hard they shattered when dropped, and candy wrappers that were treated with a fish-oil preparation spoiled the taste of the chocolate. The Uihlein's candy did not make Milwaukee famous.

Motoring through Canada's Sioux Locks on a two-week
trip to Lake Superior in 1916.

A quiet anchorage in Nipigon, on the north shore of Lake Superior.

The hills surrounding the anchorage
afford the *Wendameen's* crew a perfect view of their schooner. The figure
on the left is owner Erwin Uihlein.

A windy day and a nice bow wave. The barrels probably contain extra gasoline for the engine, which would have consumed fuel at an alarming rate.

Captain Sorensen takes a break on the foredeck.

Jimmy Ellington, professional sailor. He retired from the merchant service to a life of relative ease as a hand aboard the *Wendameen*. Here he looks for a buoy in the dwindling light.

The Indian guide.

Lunchtime guests. At center is Rudy Pabst, far left is Erwin Uihlein. In the background, wearing a hat, is Captain Sorensen. The women are locals.

Climbing aloft is no easy task without ratlines, but this unknown guest managed to get himself up the 55' foremast with his bare hands and a good pair of sneakers.

Wet weather and some hearty sailors. The *Wendameen's* first binnacle is clearly shown.

Fred Pabst, slightly pickled.

Ghosts of the cockpit. A nighttime game of cards is interrupted for a photo opportunity. Erwin Uihlein is in the back, with the white hat and pipe. Fred Pabst is closest to the table, while his brother Rudy is behind and to the left. Bill Brumder is on the far right.

The card game continues the next day, with Capt. Sorensen at the wheel.

Jimmy Ellington sits in one of the *Wendameen's* launches while it hangs in the davits. A gallon of open paint is by his side. We can see the top of a paintbrush in his right hand.

More rigging monkeys in the main crosstrees. The mainmast is 75' from step to cap.

Catching naps in the stern. Center is Auggie Pabst, with Bill Brumder to his left in the *H* sweater. Bill Brumder is the nephew of Robert and Erwin Uihlein.

Jimmy Ellington takes the helm on a blustery day. Just aft of the open skylight where the gramophone usually sat is the hand-cranked foghorn.

Loading pond ice for the galley. Just above the life ring on the right is the electric searchlight.

The *Wendameen* heads home at the end of a two-week cruise. The dory is swung in over the deck so that the schooner could lie alongside the rough stone walls of the Sioux Locks. Just to the left of the open hatch sits the Victor gramophone.

Paul L'Amoreaux
The Chicago years

Paul L'Amoreaux Jr. captioned this photo:"My pop as I remember him best." His father was well known for his favorite torn wool T-shirt.

The item appeared in the 1923 *Lake Michigan Yachting News*: "*Wendameen*, big sister of our flagship, *Rainbow,* arrived in Chicago Harbor off the Granite Park Club House Sunday evening, September 17, flying the Chicago Yacht Club burgee, a 22-foot "homeward bound" pennant, and the pennant of her new owners Messrs. K. R. Beak, Eugene L. Garey, and Paul L'Amoreaux.

"*Wendameen* was bought by her new owners from Robert and Erwin Uihlein of the Milwaukee Yacht Club with the special purpose in view of winning the next Mackinac Cup Race.

"The NEWS wants to congratulate the new owners of the *Wendameen.* None had any sailing experience previous to this season. When they joined the CYC they decided that they would learn sailing. Their first object was a boat. Hank Grebe was commissioned to buy them a boat. He had just completed the sale of *Esperanza* to Albert Pack for the estate of the late Wm. J. Starr. Pack still had on his hands the handsome little auxiliary schooner *Nokomis.*

"After sailing *Nokomis* these enterprising young men decided that they wanted a bigger boat.

" 'I would prefer to buy a boat not now on the roster of the Chicago Yacht Club,' Mr. Garey told Grebe. 'We want to help build up the Chicago YC fleet, so look elsewhere for her than Chicago, even if you have to go Down East [to Maine]. We want either a big schooner or a big yawl: fast, able and with accommodations for ourselves and our friends.'

"Grebe knew that the Uihleins were planning to build a 100' schooner, and were trying to sell *Wendameen.* The matter was broached and the sale closed on Saturday, September 16. The next morning, *Wendameen* started for Chicago on the tail end of a northeast gale that had sent big steamers scurrying into Milwaukee Harbor for refuge.

"*Wendameen* made a fast trip under a falling breeze and anchored off the downtown clubhouse in time for dinner Sunday evening, having run the more than eighty miles in under ten hours.

"The lines of the *Wendameen* are very fine, and she shows speed even under light weather conditions. With a breeze she develops splendid speed and should be a real contender in next year's Mackinac Cup Race. She is all ship, from stem to stern, and the C.Y.C. is to be congratulated on her acquisition."

**Under her new owners and now painted yacht white,
the *Wendameen* enjoys a cruise in the summer of 1924.**

**Paul L'Amoreaux stands next to part-
ner Gene Geary aboard their newly
purchased schooner yacht *Wendameen* in the fall of 1923.**

The *Wendameen*'s new owners were lawyers and business partners, but in the Chicago of the 1920s, alliances changed quickly. A year after purchasing the *Wendameen*, in 1924, "a major fisticuffs" broke out at Beak's office between Beak, Garey, and L'Amoreaux. Beak, recently indicted for fraud, was filing for bankruptcy. Garey and L'Amoreaux were representing his creditors. An argument between Garey and Beak over missing assets, including fifteen new suits and $5,000 worth of booze, turned violent.

According to the *Chicago Tribune*: "The battle royal, during which furniture was smashed, glass doors shattered and office equipment strewn about the floors, resulted, the parties said, from an attempt to settle some of the tangles of the Beak bankruptcy case 'out of court.'"

L'Amoreaux walked in on this melee, followed by another attorney and, allegedly, two paid sluggers. Beak's reported injuries included a broken nose, a fractured arm, and broken ribs. In later years, L'Amoreaux's son, Paul Jr., recounted his father's version of the incident: L'Amoreaux had entered the office just after Beak had thrown a red inkwell in Garey's face. L'Amoreaux, mistaking the ink for blood, punched Beak in the nose. The following year, Beak was no longer a partner in the *Wendameen*.

The schooner entered her first Mackinac Race in 1924. The 320-mile course on Lake Michigan, running from Chicago to Mackinac Island, was a favorite of hard-core yachtsmen. Though the *Wendemeen* did not win, she made a good showing and gave the more serious racing boats a run for their money. One hero of the race was Fritz, the cook. He had fifteen hungry crewmen on board, and from day one, though the schooner was close-hauled and heeling twenty degrees, he managed to put on feast after feast. According to the schooner's log, the first night's menu was "iced cantaloupe, cream of tomato soup, roast veal, baked potato, fresh corn, combination salad, and hot apple pie with plenty of good coffee." After dinner, with the wind coming astern, the crew enjoyed cigars, cigarettes, pipes, and a radio concert.

On the second night, the race had one of the most exciting finishes in the history of Lake Michigan yachting. From the log of the *Wendameen*, here is the account:

"We got our spinnaker and balloon off just before it hit us. A spanking squall out of the northeast.

"Forward our lookout sleeps calmly throughout it. Marty has made a record as a sleeper. The crew runs all over him to get down the light stuff but still he sleeps. The old Wendy bows to the breeze like she was tickled to death with it, and off we go down the straights like a train of express cars. With all working canvas, main tops'l and Yankee, we sure are moving some. *Josephine* is left far behind. *Vanadis* drops astern like she was tied to a mooring.

"Brad unbuttoned his shirt and, mounting the poop, declaimed: 'Stranger, thar's wind in them thar clouds,' and was nearly swept overboard. We had to give him a dram to steady his nerves.

"We passed green lights and we passed red lights. One boat, fearful we might run her down, fired a flare so we could be sure to avoid her. The shore breeze brought out lighting bugs by the millions. Our champion lookout, at last awakened, roared at us every time he saw a lightning bug until the skipper at the wheel thought we were passing through a fleet of a million ships.

"The skipper said it blew forty. The lookout said a hundred, but whatever it was, it blew. Got the tops'l off and then the Yankee just before crossing the line at 12:07. Then we rounded up and stripped her to the fores'l and came into

Fritz the cook, hero of the 1924 Mackinac Race.

the anchorage. Black as the mouth o'Hell and we couldn't tell the shore lights from the lights of the boats at anchor. Made an anchorage east of the main fleet, with two hooks down, but she was dragging.

"It was a busy night. Tired and happy we ended one of the most remarkable Mackinac Cup races on record. And ere we end, we devote a line to the 'best crew that ever jibed a forty-foot spinnaker pole seventeen times in half as many hours.' To the best seagoing chef that ever fed a hungry crew until they could eat no more, and to the valiant owners who, in the midst of the heaviest squall, knelt solemnly on the canted deck and prayed for 'a wind that'd blow the rags right off of her.' "

The *Wendameen* made a superb showing in the following year's race. Even with light winds, she finished in the top six out of fifty-two serious competitors. Plans were made to enter her in the seven-hundred-mile Bermuda race. She would be brought back east to Maine and given a complete refit, including the best sails money could buy. But the plans were never realized. In 1925, Gene Garey enjoyed one more race aboard the *Wendameen* before moving to New York, and Paul L'Amoreaux became sole owner of the schooner.

Though the *Wendameen* entered the Mackinac every year until her departure from the Great Lakes in 1933, she never won in her class. As already noted, the boat was built as a heavy cruising schooner, and though fast, she could not get ahead of the spry, light-winded racing yachts she had to compete against. She also was dragging a huge three-foot propeller underwater, which held her back further. Still, the Alden schooner was an impressive sight and always made the front page of the papers at the start of each race. When the wind blew hard, the *Wendameen* gave the others a run for their money.

The vessel's career almost ended dramatically in the mid-twenties. Paul L'Amoreaux Jr. tells this story: "I remember sitting in a coffee shop in Manitowoc, Wisconsin, when I was about eleven or twelve, and running outside to see what was burning after the fire engines went whooping past. It was, of course, *Wendameen* and she was gutted. They said it was a bilge-gas explosion.

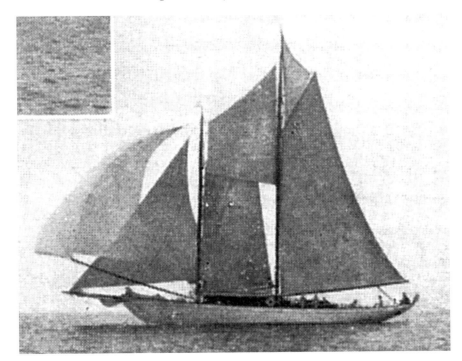

The *Wendameen* runs downwind in light air under a cloud of canvas. The sails starting at the bow are: the spinnaker, Yankee jib, foresail and mainsail. Above the foresail is the fisherman staysail, and above the mainsail is the topsail. There were other sails she could set if conditions changed. In all the *Wendameen* carried an inventory of twelve sails.

A very dashing Paul Pfeiffer.

"When she was rebuilt, the insurance company outfitted her with satin bedspreads, deep-pile wool carpeting, and absolutely exquisite Swedish crystal . . . some con job on someone by someone else (we'd been drinking from jelly glasses). But most of it vanished the first day of our return voyage to Chicago, when we ran into the helluva blow. Out of three dozen of each size of juice, highball, wine, water goblets, and ice teas, we had no more than eight of any one size by the next morning . . . and the transom skylights leaked like sieves all over the bedspreads and carpets, and the whole boat smelled of wet wool for weeks.

"Frankly I was more concerned for my chronic mal-de-mer, which was going like a fire hose for most of the voyage—egged on, as I thought I was beginning to recover, by the soda-acid, tank-type fire extinguisher in the main companionway. The acid apparently slopped over as *Wendameen* plunged, and the hose of the extinguisher started whipping around like a snake gone amok. Sure enough it squirted me right in the face. The smell was awful, and I went for the rail once more . . . and again . . . and again . . . and again. . . ."

In the summer of 1928, a lonely German immigrant named Paul Pfeiffer was walking along the Chicago waterfront. He was twenty-five years old and had just arrived in the States. He knew enough English to find a job as a machinist in a tool-and-die shop but had little opportunity to meet people. Pfeiffer had done a lot of sailing back home, so he found himself drawn to the water. As he walked along the sun-drenched harbor on a quiet Saturday morning, he saw a number of people boarding a motor launch.

In halting English he struck up a conversation and was invited to accompany the boat's occupants on a trip out to the white schooner moored beyond the channel. He hoped that he would be introduced to the owner and asked to crew for the day. In the commotion of coming alongside the schooner, the boat's occupants neglected to introduce Pfeiffer to the owner. The lack of an introduction, however, did not stop Pfeiffer from climbing aboard and making himself at home.

The schooner had been underway several hours in a pleasant breeze when the vessel's owner, Paul L'Amoreaux, approached the stranger. The immigrant was chatting away with other guests, when L'Amoreaux, with a firm hand on the stranger's shoulder, said, "So . . . who are you?" Thus began Pfeiffer's life-long friendship with the L'Amoreaux family and his love affair with the *Wendameen*. Fortunately for future generations, Pfeiffer always had a camera on board. His photographs inspired the schooner's restoration sixty years later.

From that time on, the *Wendameen* rarely got underway without Pfeiffer on board. The 1928 Mackinac Race was approaching, and the immigrant had proven himself to be such a useful hand that L'Amoreaux invited him along for the three-day race. The event almost cost Pfeiffer his job as a machinist. Perhaps it was his uncertainty with English that caused him to believe he would only be gone for a week.

After the race, when the schooner continued to head north, Pfeiffer realized he was in trouble. When the *Wendameen* entered Canadian waters, he knew he would not be at work for a long time. The trip into Canada at the end of the race was customary for L'Amoreaux. With Prohibition in effect, and Canada so near to the finish line, the owner of the *Wendameen* made this annual excursion across the border to stock up with a year's supply of liquor.

A month later, Pfeiffer returned to work, went straight to his bench, and—without a word—began to pack up his tools. He thought for sure he was now unemployed. His boss, Mr. Larsen, who was very fond of Pfeiffer, had to assure him that he could, in fact, keep his job.

It is early morning, midsummer 1928. Paul L'Amoreux is still in his bathrobe. His mistress, Tillie Beene, is just visible on the port side as she reads the paper. It is an old edition, for they are anchored in Georgian Bay, far from civilization.

It is late summer at Nevins Shipyard on City Island. The _Wendameen_ is one of the first boats hauled out for the season, and her sails are still bent. Paul L'Amoreaux had yet to meet his untimely death when this picture was taken.

Paul L'Amoreaux went back to his law firm. Although he worked on the edge of Chicago's nefarious underworld, he was never a part of it. His son Paul recalls that he and his father once ran into mob boss Al Capone at a Chicago golf course. When they were out of earshot of the famous gangster, twelve-year-old Paul turned to his father and said, "He doesn't seem like such a bad man." His father responded with a slap to the back of the boy's head and quietly added, "I never want to hear you say that again."

In 1929 the Depression began. L'Amoreaux, who had wisely avoided investing on margin, survived the stock-market crash. His friends were not as fortunate. One family story tells of the evening a well-dressed and dapper acquaintance of L'Amoreaux's came to visit. Taking the man into another room, L'Amoreaux closed the door. Several minutes later, the gentleman emerged with tears in his eyes, said goodnight to everyone, and went away. L'Amoreaux had given the acquaintance money to feed his family and had told him that if he came by the office the next day he would have a job.

By the early 1930s Paul L'Amoreaux's vigorous lifestyle was starting to catch up to him. Though still in his early forties he was cautioned by a concerned doctor to take it easy. At the end of 1932, L'Amoreaux realized that he had to give up sailing, but he did not want to forego yachting entirely. He decided to bring the _Wendameen_ to New York for one last summer. He planned to sell her at the end of the season and replace her with a motor yacht, whose operation would be less physically demanding.

In the spring of 1933, preparation was made for the schooner's return trip to the East. She was dry-docked at the Palmer Johnson Shipyard in Sturgeon Bay, Wisconsin. There she received several new planks, a new propeller and shaft, and a fresh coat of paint. After launching, with the old crew aboard (L'Amoreaux, his son, Pfeiffer, and old Jimmy Ellington, whose career on the _Wendameen_ dated back to 1915), the schooner headed across the Great Lakes, through the Erie locks, and into salt water once again. With "Chicago" still painted on her stern, she passed the summer cruising the familiar waters of Long Island Sound from a base at the Knickerbocker Yacht Club in Port Washington, New York. During that summer, world-famous maritime photographer Morris Rosenfeld captured the _Wendameen_ on film for her owner.

By now, Paul Pfeiffer was working as paid crew aboard the _Wendameen_. While in New York, his interest in all things nautical led him to scour the waterfront. Pfeiffer's wanderings took him to Manhattan's lower west side, where he was drawn to a tired old wooden sailing ship, no longer a common sight in a modern New York Harbor. On board, much to his surprise, he found himself face to face with Count Luckner, the famous "Sea Devil."

Commander Felix Graf von Luckner was born to German nobility but had run away to sea at an early age to make his own way in the world. Luckner had become a captain by the outbreak of the First World War and had convinced the German admiralty to allow him to outfit a captured steel sailing ship as a ruse of war. That vessel, which he named *Seeadler,* had the outward appearance of a Norwegian windjammer but, in fact, was equipped with cannons and a large crew. Luckner became famous for his exploits, which included the capture of sixteen enemy ships without causing the death of a single Allied sailor. Luckner was the seagoing equivalent of the Red Baron, and when the war ended, he was honored by both sides.

Now, Luckner was in the United States trying to establish a sailing academy for boys. Pfeiffer and his hero talked of home and life in America. Luckner offered to have the *Wendameen* spend the winter alongside his vessel, proclaiming he would love the company. But the Alden schooner did not raft up with the count. She would spend the winter—and the next fifty-one years—in storage.

Toward the end of summer in 1933, while visiting City Island, Paul Pfeiffer met yacht broker Gerald Ford, who had the perfect motorboat for L'Amoreaux, a sixty-footer named *Maribel.* After some discussion and negotiation, L'Amoreaux decided to sell the *Wendameen* and buy the *Maribel.* Pfeiffer was happily surprised when Mr. Ford gave him a commission check for $350.

That fall, just after the sale of the *Wendameen,* L'Amoreaux brought the schooner to Nevins Shipyard in City Island to be hauled for a survey. According to his son, he and his father were in the *Wendameen*'s saloon, removing the lead ballast from under the cabin sole so the surveyor could look underneath. It was strenuous work. Weighing fifty pounds apiece, each lead pig had to be carried up the companionway ladder and laid carefully on deck. There were five tons of ballast to move.

During the course of the day, the senior L'Amoreaux suffered nine angina attacks, which he had never experienced before, so he attributed the pain to his ulcer. Finally the pain was so severe he got a doctor to come to the schooner that night. Before the physician arrived, L'Amoreaux had drunk a fifth of Scotch to calm the pain. He was removed by ambulance and taken to his apartment in New York City, where he died the next morning. He was forty-five years old.

Shortly afterward, Paul Pfeiffer made a home for himself in Port Washington, New York. In 1935 he met a young woman named Frieda, and five years later they were married. They subsequently had three children. Pfeiffer named his first boat *Wendameen* and was happy well into his nineties. The young Paul L'Amoreaux returned to Chicago and became a lawyer just like his father. Both Pfeiffer and L'Amoreaux lived to see the *Wendameen* restored.

In April 1990 six photographs arrived from Dottie Christoffel Shelow. She had seen a *Wendameen* story in her local Florida paper and remembered having some pictures in an old box. She sent them along with this note: "My father, Dan Christoffel, is at the helm of the *Wendameen* with son James, born 1919, and with daughter Evelyn, left side of picture, born 1912 . . . and possibly my mother, Bertha, standing. Dad was the ship's mechanic. When [*Wendameen* owner] Gene Geary moved to Manhattan, our family moved to Forest Hills, Long Island, in the fall of 1924. Dad (Dan) was his chauffeur. He kept Gene's Lincoln (license #C-87) at our home. Presumably dad's position lasted until the 'crash.' It gives me pleasure to think that after all these years someone would be interested in these pictures. Enjoy, good luck, Dottie."

A view of the cockpit from the main crosstrees.

The caption from this 1924 Mackinaw news photo read, "The *Wendameen* sailed a hard race in the schooner division." Sticking well out to starboard is the 40' spinnaker pole.

Noted Paul Jr., ". . .The mugger is me. . . . I'm so proud . . ." In a photo taken about 1924, the crew has gathered around the engine room hatch. Young Paul is of, course, the kid with the wide-open mouth. Proudly behind him is his
father, and the woman behind him is Mrs. L'Amoreaux, who is described by the family as looking very much like

Charlie, cook aboard the *Wendameen* from 1928 to 1933.

When this picture was taken in the mid '20s, Jimmy Ellington was known as Old Jimmy. Paul L'Amoreaux wrote a story about Jimmy's hardships as captain aboard a merchant schooner during a winter storm in which the vessel was almost lost. He closes the narrative with ". . . and Jimmy jammed another load into his old pipe and scuttled off to polish a mess of brass. Because Jimmy's sailing master of a yacht now."

Jimmy Ellington shows off the catch of the day, which hangs proudly from the main boom.

A hot day calls for a swim. But not all the crew are skilled at the sport.

Paul Jr wrote, ". . . All these from Lake Superior. My dad caught a 48-pound lake trout that was, coincidentally, 48" long." Above the unfortunate fish, mounted on the rail, is the *Wendameen*'s signal cannon.

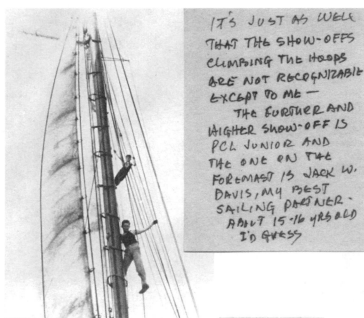

IT'S JUST AS WELL THAT THE SHOW-OFFS CLIMBING THE HOOPS ARE NOT RECOGNIZABLE EXCEPT TO ME — THE FURTHER AND HIGHER SHOW-OFF IS PCL JUNIOR AND THE ONE ON THE FOREMAST IS JACK W. DAVIS, MY BEST SAILING PARTNER — ABOUT 15-16 YRS OLD I'D GUESS

Young Paul was in his seventies when he shared his album and memories. Many of the photographs had notes like this one attached.

Paul Pfeiffer at the wheel. The new binnacle is clearly visible. It replaced the original, which had been destroyed by fire. To Pfeiffer's right, just outside the cockpit, is the small picnic Victrola.

A proud Mrs. L'Amoreaux with her son Paul at the helm.

It's not the Little Rascals. A group of Paul Jr.'s friends enjoy a day of yachting. His first love, Mary Gilbert, sits far right.

According to Paul Jr., "The 'Flapper' is my mother's cousin Georgia Olsen. She is the one who made Jimmy Ellington want to quit when she did the Charleston on Jimmy's newly varnished cockpit sole." Next to Georgia Olsen are Mrs. L'Amoreaux and Paul Sr. Sitting on deck with his eyes almost covered by his hat is young Paul. There must have been music on board besides that provided by the gramophone; if you look closely under Miss Olsen's arm you'll see Paul Jr.'s kazoo.

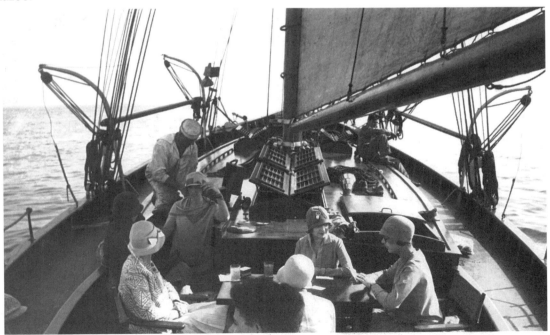

The *Wendameen* ghosts along in light winds on a port tack. Paul Pfeiffer changes a record on the gramophone as the ladies play cards in the cockpit. Mrs. L'Amoreaux stands in the main companionway.

Paul Jr. hides in the belly of the stays'l while his father sits on the rail reading the newspaper.

A lazy summer day underway. The fores'l is set on the off chance a breeze will spring up. L'Amoreaux steers while several friends nap around him.

Looking forward on the starboard side. Paul Pfeiffer sits at the forward end of the cabin with the foresheet in his hand. The cabin top, which is covered with canvas set in white lead paste to keep the accommodations below dry, is starting to wrinkle.

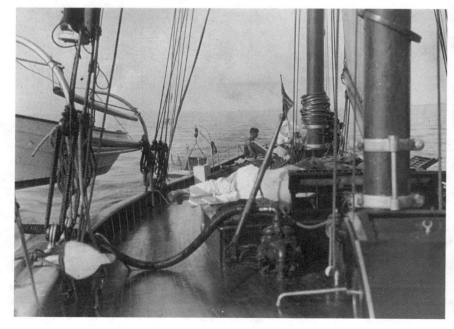

Looking aft down the starboard side. The object in the foreground with the long hose and wood handle is the bilge pump. Many photos show that by the late 1920s it was always rigged and ready to use.

The Great Lakes can get rough. Paul Pfeiffer had to hold onto the leach (after edge) of the mainsail with his knees to take this photograph.

Mrs. L'Amoreaux takes the helm. Judging by some expressions, this was a novelty.

Paul L'Amoreaux has a noontime dance with Tillie Beene, the other woman in his life. On a Sunday drive with Mrs. L'Amoreaux and Paul Jr., Mr. L'Amoreaux absentmindedly made a turn off the main road. As they drove along a side street young Paul asked, "Dad, where are we going?" His father pulled the car over and said he wasn't sure. Then Mrs. L'Amoreaux spoke up, "You know perfectly well." Pointing to an apartment building across the street, she added, "Your mistress, Tillie Beene, lives on the second floor of that house."

Motoring along in a calm with the canopy rigged to stave off the hot sun. An unidentified woman is steering a compass course while another studies a chart.

Classic bathing beauties . . .

. . . the three were inseparable.

The water was deep enough by the shore in Georgian Bay that the *Wendameen* was able to tie up to the trees.

The Chicago years • 41

The *Wendameen*'s sailing dory.

The *Wendameen* tows a small sloop through the Wells Street bridge on the Chicago River. The man in the hatch is the engineer. Next to him, a crew member stands ready to relay any orders that L'Amoreaux, who is at the helm, might give. Things could get tricky because once the engineer was below, he could barely hear commands over the noise of the engine.

Paul Pfeiffer discovered that Count Luckner was a guest aboard the *U.S.S. Wilmette*. He took this picture thinking that would be the closest he ever got to his hero. Little did he know that five years later, in 1933, he would meet the count in New York and the two would become friends. The *Wilmette* was originally a civilian steam ferry from Chicago named the *Eastland*. In 1915 that vessel capsized, killing 850 people. She was raised and then purchased by the U.S. Navy for use as a gunboat.

The *Wendameen* had a collision with a docked ferry while trying to maneuver into this V-shaped berth. Her gas motor, controlled by an engineer below, was not taken out of gear in time to avoid the schooner's going headlong into the slip. The *Wendameen*'s crew are at her bow inspecting the damage. The ferry crew stares at the troubled yacht. Before the summer was over, Paul L'Amoreaux had engine controls placed in the cockpit.

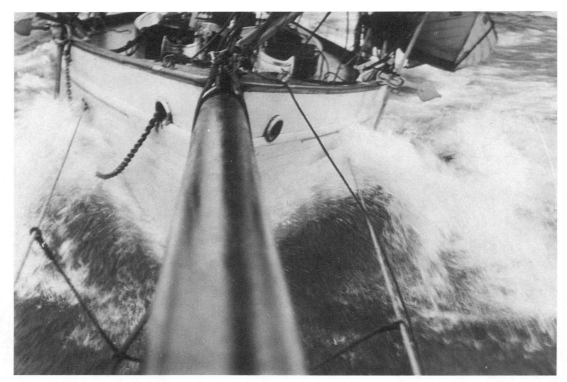

Sailing with "a bone in her teeth."

It's blowing better than twenty-five knots, but the captain sees no need to reef the mains'l.

The wind continues to build. The mains'l has been taken down and is just visible furled on the boom. The *Wendameen* works to windward under fores'l and stays'l. This is the same sail combination that so impressed John Alden aboard the schooner *Fame* on his trip of 1909. Just inside the hatch is the infamous fire extinguisher that went off in Paul Jr.'s face.

The *Wendameen* at the start of the 1928 Mackinac Race. The big ketch *Vanadis* comes up from leeward.

An entry in the schooner's log reads, "The Wendy bows to the breeze like she's been tickled to death with it, and off we go like a train of express cars!" Here the *Wendameen* battles the ketch *Dorello* on July 27, 1929. The photo appeared in that Saturday's edition of the *Chicago Daily News.*

Here the *Wendameen* is in Canada. The whole crew pitches in to unload cases of liquor labeled "Highland Queen" and bring them aboard.

Bottles from Paul L'Amoreaux's private stock wait by the *Wendameen*'s cockpit for safe storage below.

Paul Jr. described this scene as follows, ". . . in Palmer Johnson's yard in Sturgeon Bay, Wisconsin . . . the perch fishing was wonderful, no matter where you dropped your line. . . . " The *Wendameen* is hauled in a huge dry dock during the spring of 1933. Preparations were made here for her return trip to the East. Looking under the schooner's stern we see that the horn timber has been replaced. She also received several planks, as well as a new propeller and propeller shaft.

The *Wendameen* has sailed back across the lakes to Buffalo, New York. Her masts have been removed so that she can again navigate under the low bridges of the Erie barge canal. The mainmast has been laid across two hefty sawhorses, and the foremast will soon have its weight on deck, as well.

The rigging seems like a tangled mess, but it will all go back together when the *Wendameen* reaches Albany. The weight of all the gear is about five tons.

Sailing from Port Washington, the *Wendameen* heads toward City Island, New York, which is just visible on the horizon. She will spend the next fifty-three years there.

Rosenfeld Collection

It is now early autumn. The *Wendameen's* fores'l and mains'l hang loosely about her deck, drying before they are removed for storage. Paul L'Amoreaux has passed away, and the job of laying up his schooner falls on his old friends and crew. Just saying goodbye to Captain L'Amoreaux would have been sad, but more so because the *Wendameen* had to be left behind.

A gentle west wind dries the mains'l as Paul Pfeiffer looks astern from the *Wendameen's* dry perch. He can see across the waters of Long Island Sound to Port Washington, where he will soon make his home.

Under cover and ready for a long sleep . . .

Gerald W. Ford
The forgotten decades

For most of prosperous America, the world came crashing down on Black Tuesday, October 24, 1929. The affluence of the 1920s had increasingly become a paper tiger. From 1919 to 1929, corporate America had bloomed. Twelve hundred mergers had consumed more than six thousand independent companies. By 1929, two hundred corporations controlled almost 50 percent of American industry.

During that period, labor productivity increased an astounding 43 percent. However, average American workers did not see wages rise significantly, and so could not afford to buy the goods they produced. Banks aggressively financed business expansion and land speculation. During this frenzy, bank managers became increasingly corrupt and made loans without security, especially to companies where bank officers held interests. One banker at the time said, "We provided everything for the customers but a roulette wheel."

In 1929, almost overnight, banks failed by the hundreds. Within a few

World-renowned yacht broker G. W. Ford, from the 1922 Ford Agency catalog.

WE SOLICIT YOUR BUSINESS IN THE
PURCHASE, SALE, AND CHARTER OF YACHTS

GERALD W. FORD

years, ninety thousand businesses went bankrupt. Fifteen million people, a quarter of the labor force, were out of work. Those who still had jobs saw their wages drop by almost 50 percent. Agricultural prices sank to their lowest level since the Civil War, and thousands of family farms were lost. Many Americans could not afford to eat. Never before had such hunger and poverty been known in the United States.

One of those who survived the Depression was Gerald W. Ford, the New York yacht broker who was to engineer the sale of the *Wendameen* and the purchase of the *Maribel* in 1933.

The Ford Yacht Agency had opened after the end of the First World War. The company had a wealthy clientele and prospered during the '20s, when free spending was rampant. Known to be financially conservative, Ford himself survived the market crash. In 1933, during the depths of the Depression, he purchased the twenty-one-year-old *Wendameen* from Fredrick L. Richards of New York, who had owned her less than a year.

Shortly afterward, Ford advertised the schooner for $8,000; location: Nevins Shipyard, City Island, New York. The economy and other factors dictated that she would not sell for what the broker was asking. For one thing, the *Wendameen* was now showing her age from years of sailing the fresh waters of the Great Lakes, where there was no salt to preserve her timbers.

Ford also listed the schooner for charter, but still there was no market. Though prices had fallen—milk was ten cents a quart; steak, twenty-nine cents a pound; and a new home, $3,000—the average American was having trouble buying the basics. The truly wealthy who had survived the crash preferred new and more modern yachts, and had no interest in the small and aging *Wendameen*. In 1934 Ford received one low offer. However, he was becoming attached to the pretty little schooner. He planned a cruise to the West Indies on the *Wendameen*, but the trip never came about. By that time, the schooner was no longer seaworthy.

City Island, a tiny speck at the mouth of Long Island Sound, just north of the Bronx, was one of the hubs of world yachting. Its craftsmen were renowned for producing all manner of boats and yachts by the thousands. Nevins was one of its more prestigious yards. In 1936, Ford hired two shipwrights to replace many of the *Wendameen*'s aging timbers. He arranged for them to work on her when there were no other jobs available. While the restoration was going on, Ford listed the schooner for sale at $15,000, stating that the boat would be completed and ready to sail.

The cover of the 1922 Ford catalog. The sixty-five-page book contained a sampling of some of the yachts his company offered for sale. They ranged from gas runabouts and cabin cruisers to 250' steam yachts and sailing vessels.

Suddenly, the repair work came to a halt. On September 21, 1938, a surprise hurricane devastated the eastern seaboard. With winds of up to a hundred and fifty miles per hour, waves fifty feet high, and a storm surge of seventeen feet above normal high tide, it caused seven hundred deaths. The hurricane of '38 destroyed or damaged close to twenty thousand houses, leaving sixty-three thousand people homeless. The damage totaled $6.2 million in 1938 dollars.

Close to half of that was in the loss of boats, docks, marine equipment, and shorefront facilities. The western side of City Island was completely shattered. Fortunately, Nevins Shipyard was located on the east side of the island, and the *Wendameen* was spared. After the hurricane, thousands of people traveled to New York and New England for jobs in clean-up, repair, and reconstruction. The heavily insured yachts and shipyards on City Island now required a skilled

These pictures, taken between 1936 and 1938, illustrate the extensive rebuild Mr. Ford started on the *Wendameen*. By the time the work was put on hold, 60 percent of her frames and planks had been replaced. The mainmast was still stepped at this time, though the foremast had been removed. The dark patches on her bows show where rotten wood has been dug out of the bulwarks. This area had still not been repaired by 1961.

labor force to rebuild or replace the boats and property damaged by the storm. Ford's part-timers were no longer available to finish the *Wendameen*. The Great Hurricane had ended the Great Depression in the Northeast.

That same year, another storm was brewing. On September 1, Germany invaded Poland, and the world was again at war. Though the United States was not yet involved, this tempest ended the Depression for the rest of the country. On City Island, the outbreak of the conflict began a strange hiatus for the *Wendameen,* one that was to last for the next half-century.

The First World War was still fresh in Ford's memory. He had seen the Navy requisition private sailing vessels for submarine patrol and reduce their rigs to an inglorious minimum so the sails could be managed by a small, inexperienced crew. The boats were painted battleship gray from end to end and sent out in even the harshest conditions to patrol the coast for enemy submarines. These "mystery ships" made no noise underway, and therefore could not easily be detected by the submerged enemy. They were hard used, and many were in such horrible shape after the war that their owners would not take them back. Ford did not want the same fate for his schooner. He sensed that it was only a matter of time before the United States became involved in the European conflict. Therefore, Ford kept the *Wendameen* unfinished, without engine or masts.

Earlier in 1938, Col. George Patton had commissioned a schooner from John Alden. Knowing the United States would soon be brought into the European conflict, he named the vessel *When and If* because he planned to sail around the world "when and if" he returned home.

Meanwhile, when the United States finally entered the war in 1941, Ford contributed the *Wendameen*'s five tons of lead ballast, which Paul L'Amoreaux and his son had so laboriously removed years earlier, to be used for making ammunition. Many yachts gave up their ballast during this time. The *Wendameen* remained laid up throughout the Second World War, and when the

Nevins Shipyard, 1961. The *Wendameen* is forty-one years old and is still holding her shape. Her neighbor to port is a 12-meter *America*'s Cup contender.

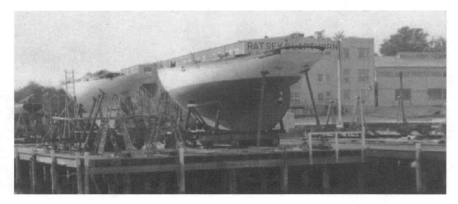

A second view in the same year. The *Wendameen* sits in an old-style yacht cradle. These were moved around the yard along narrow-gauge tracks as vessels were hauled and launched. The large building beyond the *Wendameen* is the famous sail loft of Ratsey and Lapthorn. It had made the schooner's original suit of a dozen sails. Here, the top planks of the *Wendameen*'s transom are missing. They had been removed but not replaced during the 1936 rebuild.

Yet another perspective from 1961. The *Wendameen* is showing her age after years of neglect and despite the earlier repairs. The schooner has been out of commission for twenty-eight years. Mr. Ford stands with his back to the camera. Within two years Nevins was out of business.

conflict finally ended and prosperity returned, Ford was too busy to spend time on the schooner he had grown to love.

The Ford Yacht Agency was fully engaged in finding boats for the soldiers, sailors, and officers who—like George Patton—had spent five long years in hopes of coming home to the American dream.

By the 1950s, Ford's plans for the *Wendameen* now involved keeping her for his retirement. The schooner remained untouched and in storage at Nevins Shipyard. Many of the repairs performed in the 1930s, as well as untouched areas of the schooner, were starting to decay. Under an increasingly leaky cover, with poor ventilation and summer heat, the old *Wendameen* was beginning to rot—again. In the early 1960s, Nevins closed its doors. By now the *Wendameen* had been out of commission for thirty years. Her stagnation was starting to become legendary as her condition worsened.

Ford had the schooner launched and moved to another reputable shipyard on City Island, Minnefords, which was then engaged in building *America*'s Cup contenders.

At age sixty-five, Gerald Ford decided it was time again to breathe life into his *Wendameen*. He allowed the shipyard to pick away at projects on board when there was no other work for the men. This saved him money, but it made progress very slow. In 1974, many bottom planks and the rotten wooden keel were replaced. But now the schooner's deck was deteriorating, and her interior was partially gutted. Many items of value had been stolen, including her wheel, so Ford had everything else removed, such as bronze portholes and hardware, and all such items were placed in storage for safekeeping.

As work continued off and on through the '70s, the craftsmanship became sloppier. Workers and visitors at the yard knew the *Wendameen* was once a beautiful vessel, but she was now a mockery. Everyone believed she would not sail again. Out of comission for forty years, the schooner was witnessing her familiar world slip away. Nearby, where Nevins Shipyard had been, there was a new elementary school and park. Even the *Wendemeen* was not exempt from changes. In trying to keep up with modern times, Ford planned to alter her rig and make her into a ketch. He had some used masts and sails for the purpose; in his mind, there was no place in yachting for an old-fashioned gaff-rigged schooner.

But vessels like the *Wendameen* did have their followers. As fiberglass replaced wood in the boating world, a movement of staunch traditionalists started to grow. One young foundling member of that movement was a seventeen-year-old deckhand aboard an old skipjack-turned-yacht that was hauled out for repairs at Minnefords.

Neal Parker
Converging lines

Neal Parker as a seventeen-year-old deckhand.

It was a hot summer day in '74. I was squeezed under the damp bottom planking of the old 56' skipjack *Mamie A. Mister.* A pair of scuffed cowboy boots appeared by the bilge next to my shoulder. It was Dr. Carl Beam, the boat's owner. He was wandering around looking for any distraction that would keep him from having to pick up a paintbrush. "Let's take a break," he said. "I want to show you something."

I tossed my brush into a can of gasoline to keep it soft. We walked across Minnefords Boat Yard as Carl told me a great story: "There's a schooner hauled out nearby, been out for about fifty years. This guy who owns her is in his eighties and has never sailed her once. Just works on her." We arrived at the end of the shipyard. There, in a partially open metal shed, was a big white schooner. I thought my eyes were deceiving me; though she was a terrible mess, I had never seen a more shapely hull.

We walked around her. Her garboard planks were off, and so were some others. There was new wood in her keel with red-lead paint slathered about. It was hard to step back and look at her in the building, but standing close and looking up, she seemed to go on forever. This boat was quite a contrast to the flat old *Mamie Mister.* Carl chewed on his unlit pipe as we both looked lovingly at the schooner. Then, from the bright daylight at the far end of the shed, a form took shape. Carl, who was about sixty, said, "That's old Gerry Ford."

The slightly hunched figure was carrying a small kit bag. He probably saw us but paid no attention. At eighty-something, Ford was probably used to people gawking at his schooner. He positioned himself to climb the long, red-primed ladder that was leaning against the port quarter. Carl let out an introductory cough. Mr. Ford then looked deliberately in our direction. "Hey Gerry, just showing the kid around . . . okay to come up?" I don't remember Ford's acknowledgment, but I was next up the ladder, with Carl close astern.

Eventually, Carl and I went back to work. We painted the *Mamie*'s bottom—the only paint she saw on a regular basis. Carl made sure that she kept her workboat roots. She had the patina that only a seventy-year-old oyster boat could have. Carl was my mentor, and he made sure I knew that though yachts were lovely, workboats were real. The *Mamie* looked very real.

I made many visits to City Island over the years after that—by water, bus, and then car when I finally had a driver's license. Sometimes I was working, but as often as not, I was there just to look at boats. The old schooner, which I learned was named *Wendameen*, was of course a mainstay of my City Island experience.

The lovely old *Mamie*.

Gerald Ford (Mr. Ford to me) was often on board. He was a breed of owner I had become familiar with as I learned my way around the waterfront.

On regular weekends, he would go to the *Wendameen*, make his way aboard, sit in the cockpit or somewhere, and perhaps take a scraper from his bag. He might talk if someone was around. Perhaps he talked if no one was around, but then he'd scrape some wood while the rest of the boat was in helpless tatters. After a few minutes of that he would sigh, put his tool away, putter with something else, and call it a day.

I had worked for years as a mate and then captain in the Maine windjammer fleet when Carl turned the *Mamie* over to me in 1981. He let me set up a charter business in New York in exchange for maintaining his old skipjack. I sailed the boat from the foot of the Brooklyn Bridge in the summers, and Carl had use of the boat in the winter months, when the bay was less crowded. He loved sailing in the dead of winter.

At the end of my first season in New York with the *Mamie,* I purchased my first boat from a charter operator in Long Island. I was twenty-six. The *Francy* was a 42' clamming sloop and a rotten little thing. The previous owner had raised her off the bottom in Sandy Hook, where the tide had been flowing through her for years. He claimed he had refastened the vessel's planking, but as I later found out, most of the screws on her bottom were in only halfway.

She had a lovely bow and a nice sheer that ended abruptly at a rather ugly, sawed-off stern. It caused Carl to remark, "Well there's three-quarters of a nice boat." I bought the *Francy* in November, and every day for about three weeks I drove the four hours to Long Island from Brooklyn to get her ready for the trip to my dock in the East River. It was a good thing Carl had toughened me up with years of winter sailing. He and I made the trip just before Christmas.

Though the two-day journey was more memorable than eventful, I did become alarmed when we hit open water and, while looking through the *Francy*'s cargo hatch, I noticed her planking rippling along with each wave that passed beneath her. The boat sank at the dock in the East River early that spring. I raised her, sailed her a bit, and "fixed" her during the second summer that I ran charters on the *Mamie*. Carl, seeing that I was up and running, took the skipjack and left me to my own devices. I had the *Francy* for three more years.

About this time, I started looking for a bigger boat. Reading the classifieds in the *Sunday Times,* I saw that a schooner was for sale on City Island. Phoning the listed number, I found myself ear to ear with old Mr. Ford. He had the *Wendameen* for sale; price: $35,000. That was a bit out of my league, and so I wished him well and looked elsewhere for a new boat. I flew to Miami one afternoon to look at an old Gulf Coast fishing schooner. That didn't pan out either.

Finally, in the spring of '84, while the *Wendameen*'s fate was—unknown to me—being decided, I found another boat. Before I sold the *Francy,* I purchased the 84' Thames sailing barge *Ethel.* She had been launched in 1894 at Harwich, England, to carry raw linseed to markets in London. Though she was a great old workboat, even Carl thought I was a bit crazy. I bought her with the help of my leery parents. The price was right; she had just been condemned.

If the fight to save her had just involved work, I might have succeeded. Let it suffice to say that she was assuredly haunted by the most malevolent spirit I have ever met at sea or ashore. A year and a half later, the *Ethel* did get me back to Maine, where in the fall of 1986 I tricked someone into buying her. How I had longed for that day—but that's another story.

While I was busy with my *Ethel,* the *Wendameen* was forced back into the water. Early in 1984, Mr. Ford launched her when Minnefords went out of the yacht-repair business. Workers rafted her to an old railroad barge, which the yard used to protect its smaller docks. It was mid-March when a storm hit City Island, sinking the barge. Later Gerald Ford told me that the *Wendameen* had parted her lines rather than being dragged under.

Having gotten herself underway, she was driven hard aground, a rock poking through her starboard side. Her rudder was broken, and much of the stern was stove in from the pounding. Her end was at hand. But wise Mr. Ford had kept the *Wendameen* well insured. He brought her off the rocks and hauled

The poor *Francy* sank during the first spring I owned her. The wake from a passing tug crushed her fenders and thrust her against a bolt that was protruding from the dock. The resulting hole sent her to the bottom. I had her raised within twenty-four hours thanks to the help of the New York City Fire Department tugboat.

The haunted *Ethel*.

her out at Consolidated, the third big shipyard on City Island. With just enough repairs so that she could stay afloat, the *Wendameen* was relaunched.

Mr. Ford was ninety-two years old, had never sailed the schooner, and had not yet retired from the brokerage business. Finally he found a buyer. This individual managed to do still more damage with a poor attempt at repairs before he finally gave up and stuck the vessel in the mud in Darien, Connecticut. About this time representatives from three maritime museums interested in the *Wendameen* looked the schooner over on behalf of their respective foundations. Though John Alden's first yacht design was of historic significance, they all concluded that she was beyond repair.

A sailor ashore and his money are soon parted—and I was no different. With the Ethel sold and having returned to Maine, I was desperate to find another boat. Calling everyone I knew—and some I didn't—I finally spoke with a broker in Florida. I told him, "I am in the market for a big schooner." His ears perked up. "I am not afraid of work, and—oh, yes—I have $15,000 to my name."

Then he described an old 67' schooner that had been in City Island for years and was now "rumored to be dying somewhere in either Connecticut or New York or something like that. Good luck." I was sure he was describing the old *Wendameen*.

It took some doing, but at last I found her.

Neal Parker
Changing hands

Throughout history, modern man dreamed of reaching the moon. However, once we got there, we didn't go back all that much. That is the difference between wanting and having. I'd had my occasional daydreams about the *Wendameen*, but now there was a chance I might really own her.

The schooner was in the mud in Darien, Connecticut, behind the home of an elderly widow. Ruth seemed a delightful, vivacious woman. Her favorite answer to anything was, "Oh dear, I'm so old I don't even buy green bananas any more." Her home was a huge, rambling estate on the only deepwater property in a very wealthy community. I don't know how long she had been widowed, but Ruth was now estate rich and cash poor. Her once majestic house was a shadow of its former self. The grounds were unkempt, her docks and pilings were a hazard to walk on.

The inside of her home was something out of Charles Dickens's *Great Expectations*. Ruth was Miss Havisham, and for a short while I was the wide-eyed Pip. The mansion had been untouched for decades. Nature had encroached inside and out. Downstairs in the back hall she opened a refrigerator to show me a cat she didn't have the heart to bury. Over her mantel, a huge gilded frame held a portrait of a most beautiful and elegant woman. "That was me forty years

The *Wendameen* hauled out for a few days at Pilots Point Marina. It was a good chance to survey the schooner. I didn't learn anything new—she needed work.

The *Wendameen* as I found her in 1986. The view is from Ruth's window.

ago," said Ruth with a smile that was just like the one in the painting.

Outside was her real pride and joy. Ruth loved boats, and they were everywhere. Her porch held some old canoes and rowboats, both hanging and strewn about in various states of disrepair. Just beyond the front door in the tall grass was a 40' schooner called the *Gray Gull,* which had been there for twenty years or more. Elsewhere, half hauled out in a cradle at the end of her front yard was a 30' sloop. The mast was standing but twisted, the tide was running through the hull. Boats were everywhere.

Finally, outside Ruth's bedroom window, in a place of great honor, was the *Wendameen.* She was old and neglected, but still beautiful. I found my way aboard. Her bilge was full of water. I tasted it. It was fresh, so at least it was rainwater and the hull was not leaking. I looked around, sat down, and looked around some more. In the back of my mind I knew I would have to delude myself if I was going to make this work. The *Wendameen* did not have long to live.

As I had grown up and read stories about the last days of the great sailing ships, the saddest parts involved those vessels that, instead of being lost at sea in all their glory, were burned for their metal fastenings—or, worse, left to die in some backwater. I stood on the shore looking at the *Wendameen.* Her bow was just out of reach as she strained a bit at her lines. There was a chain running from her port hawsepipe to a piling. The heavy steel links crossed her stem and were chewing it into pulp. The vessel moved slightly, perhaps trying to get a bit more comfortable.

"She's in rough shape," I thought. "Hmm. I could get rid of that long cabin, and she'd look just like a fishing schooner. Carl would like that. I could stick in an engine, fix the rudder, get her to Maine, and be sailing within a year. But I have no money. . . ."

Then the *Wendameen* looked at me in despair, and a small voice said, "It will work."

The fellow I needed to see about the purchase was living on a boat nearby. He was not a pleasure to do business with, but on October 9, 1986, I gave him all my money, and he signed the schooner over to me. The *Wendameen* was now mine.

Ruth's home in Connecticut looked like the *Wendameen's* final resting place, especially when the tide was out and the mud was all around her tattered hull.

Ruth was so happy for me. She said, "Oh, keep the *Wendameen* here. You can fix her right there, and I won't charge you rent." That Ruth was a clever one. I had come to realize that she invited young men with old boats to fix them in her yard, and then when they gave up she had another relic! I cast another glance at her rotting trophies. No thanks; no way, I thought. "That's very kind," I said, "but I really have to get the schooner to Maine."

My first challenge was to pull the *Wendameen* off the mud. She was floating in a hole she had dug for herself. At high tide, using a motor launch run by the sympathetic caretaker of a nearby estate, we were able to move the schooner with ease. I tied her up to a deepwater dock and went home for the night. When I returned the next day, the *Wendameen* was back in the mud and lying on her port side. She had been towed back and left at high tide to fall over as the water went out. The fellow who had sold me the boat was changing his mind. He had also helped himself to one 250-pound anchor, a lot of chain, and a few other things, perhaps hoping I would give up and just walk away.

And there was Ruth twittering, "You can keep the boat here!" Suddenly she sounded like the witch in Hansel and Gretel. The pressure was on to move the *Wendameen.*

Some of the schooner's gear was still at Mr. Ford's home office on City Island. The day after I purchased the *Wendameen,* I got together with him. He showed me around and mentioned some of the inventory that came with the schooner. The house was filled with parts and pieces from almost a century of life in boats. Everything was tagged with a different yacht's name. In one room crowded with nautical miscellany, Mr. Ford pointed to half a dozen horsehair-filled mattresses. "These are yours," he said, brushing them with his hand as I choked from the dust. They had not been aboard since 1933. He tapped the bronze steering gear with his toe. "That, too."

In the hall he pointed to the *Wendameen*'s compass. As we moved from room to room, I felt as if I was pulling his teeth. He really didn't want to part with anything. "What about those?" I asked, pointing to some bronze letters hanging from a hook.

"No, not those," Mr. Ford said. "Those are from another boat." Not missing a beat I pointed out that they spelled N-E-E-M-A-D-N-E-W.

It was a memorable visit. Mr. Ford gave me some old photos, and we talked of the *Wendameen*. I wanted more history, but all he or anybody knew was that she had been in the Great Lakes, that she was an Alden schooner from 1912, and that he had bought her around 1933. He was convinced I would waste my time by restoring the *Wendameen*'s original rig. He had two old masts from a smaller schooner called the *Nina*. He had planned to step them in reverse to make the *Wendameen* a modern ketch. Those newer masts and sails came with the sale. He wasn't sure what happened to her original rig. (Eventually I found her foremast in an airplane hanger in the Bronx.)

It sounded as if I had a truckload of gear to move. I went back to Maine and bought a huge four-door $500 pickup truck. I planned to lay the masts on board the *Wendameen* for the trip to Maine. I arranged to return on the following Saturday. I was anxious to get my things. That same small voice told me to "rush."

That Saturday, instead of being met by Mr. Ford, I was greeted by his funeral. A car had hit Gerald W. Ford in front of his house the day before. That was his end, at the age of 93. I don't think I mourned for Mr. Ford as much as I did for my stuff. I went to my folk's house in New York to spend the night in despair. It was too soon for things to go this badly. The next day I returned to Mr. Ford's home to see what could be done. He had led a frugal life and had died wealthy. He had never married, but his house was now overrun with relations from near and far. In addition, every character on City Island came out of the woodwork to first mourn "Gerry" and then claim what he had supposedly promised to give them.

I was a complete stranger to them all. After paying my respects and pleading my case, I was invited back—but only to remove items with a *Wendameen* label.

When I showed up two days later, it was Mr. Ford's family that was in despair. He had been a pack rat. His house, two small barns, and yard were filled with tons of old, new, and used marine supplies. He even had thousands of

The schooner's starboard side, looking aft. She was a shadow of her former glory, missing decking, frames, and topside planks. The hull had actually been damaged by recent attempts at repair.

used screws, sized and sorted. His cellar was packed, as well. As we hunted about looking for *Wendameen* labels, I quickly discovered that Mr. Ford was holding out on the old schooner. We found her booms and gaffs in his yard, and her entire rig was labeled and stowed under tons of gear in his barn. All the bronze portholes were in his parlor, as well as the schooner's bell and lifeline stanchions. In his cellar was the lumber for a new cabin top. I found her electric searchlight, ice tongs, toilets, air whistle, and more.

Mr. Ford had gear from dozens of other boats, too. There were lights from this yacht, turnbuckles from that yacht, deck chairs from the '20s, and so on. The only organized items were his business records. There were some two-dozen large filing cabinets stuffed with photographs and descriptions of every boat and yacht the G. W. Ford agency had handled since World War I. It was a great and valuable collection, which the family subsequently fought over for years.

I was very careful to take only what belonged to the schooner. After several days of digging through the house, Mr. Ford's relations started to offer me as much of the miscellaneous nuts, bolts, rigging, and hardware that I could take; they were getting tired of moving things. Five truckloads later, I was finished. If Mr. Ford had not died when he did, it might not have been possible to restore the schooner. The *Wendameen* items I uncovered would have been impossible to replace.

About a month later, the caretaker and I removed the schooner from the mud again. This time we kept going—all the way to a dock in Norwalk, just a few miles to the east. It was now about a week before Thanksgiving. In the month or so since buying the *Wendameen,* I had given up on bringing her to Maine under her own power. It would have been nice to invest in an engine, but she still had no rudder or propeller, and there was no place to take her out of the water. No yard was going to haul a boat that looked as if she was ready to break in two.

I thought about hiring a small tug, but that would have cost $500 an hour for twenty-four hours. Even if it had been affordable, one look at the poor *Wendameen* would have told the tug company that there was a liability problem. I scoured the waterfront near my final destination of Camden, Maine, and along the Connecticut shore. At last I found the owner of a 50' fishing trawler in Gro-

Looking at the overhead on the starboard side of the saloon. Upper right is where the mainmast should pass through the cabin top. Along the cabin sides there were about two dozen rusty clamps holding a timber that had been fitted at least thirty years earlier but never fastened. Those clamps came in handy during the restoration.

ton, Connecticut; he was willing to take a chance, charging me $100 an hour. I could just afford twenty hours' worth of towing. If all went well, the *Wendameen* and I would be in Maine for Thanksgiving.

It was a few days before the holiday—cloudy, damp, and cold. Having met us in Norwalk, the fisherman took the Wendy and me in tow, and we headed east down Long Island Sound. There was a gentle but ominous head wind. The day reminded me of the trip I had made to Mystic Seaport when I was thirteen. That was also November. The place was empty—just my family, some ghosts, and I.

Now I was alone on the deck of my own ghost ship. The dragger was a couple of hundred feet ahead, while I remained on board as tow master of my schooner. There was no way to steer, nothing to do but man the pumps if needed. I had to watch my step as the old hull began to pitch in the open water. There were huge gaps in the rotten deck. In the places where the planking was good enough for me to stand on, the rails were gone, so there was a good chance of going over the side. Still, it was good to be underway, the end of a hawser was better than where we had been, even on such a melancholy day.

Shortly, the winds began to increase. Huge plumes of spray were flung over the *Wendameen*'s bows, and they carried aft almost her whole length— so frequently that it was more like rain than spray. I was cold and drenched right through my foul-weather gear. The *Wendameen* didn't seem to mind a bit. She was being towed at eight knots into a twenty-five-knot head wind. Over the bow I saw the crew of the dragger give the occasional thumbs up. For some time, I tried to huddle under an old plastic tarp in the cockpit. Once in a while I checked the bilge. Remarkably, I didn't have to run the pump. That was very encouraging. Shortly before dark, the captain from the dragger gave a couple of blasts on his horn to get my attention. He was altering course and turning up the Thames River to sit out the foul weather at his dock in Groton.

Once in the protection of the Connecticut shore, the wind dropped almost

Looking aft on the port side. There was a lot of new decking, but it stopped short, halfway from the bow, because the beams underneath were so rotten. Mr. Ford had the new bulwarks and rails supported by thirty-five custom-cast bronze stanchions per side.

to a calm. We were nearing Groton when there was frantic waving aboard the dragger as the crew cast me off. Their boat had lost steering, and they had to cut me loose to save themselves. The *Wendameen* and I were on our own. I moved quickly to the bow to get my anchor ready. But we never had to use it.

The *Wendameen* quietly placed herself alongside the city pier in New London, just across the river from Groton. She nudged right in as if a harbor pilot was on board. I stepped to the dock with a line. Then I heard the small voice again, "Spend the winter here." Soon the dragger was alongside, but the *Wendameen* was secure. The fishermen went home for the night and the holiday. On Monday I met with the dragger's captain. I told him I was looking for a berth in New London for the winter and would need him one more time when I found a place. He seemed glad not to have to tow the schooner all the way to Maine.

I found a ramshackle dock at the south end of town. We moved to that berth for what ended up to be the first of two winters. I had been living mostly out of my car, so it was time to find a cheap, warm place to live nearby. I knew my way around town because I had wintered there with the *Ethel* the year before. My needs were satisfied by a one-room flat above a lawyer's office in New London, just minutes away from the *Wendameen*. Winter began, and I dug in.

At this point I knew little of the schooner's past, only what Mr. Ford had told me. Since I couldn't yet restore the boat, I could at least find out more about her. I felt somehow that her future might be tied to her past. Mystic Seaport Library was only minutes away. When I looked up the *Wendameen* in the 1912 Lloyds Registry of Yachts, I came upon the first owner's name—Chester W. Bliss of Springfield, Massachusetts, homeport: New London, Connecticut! I stared at the page in disbelief. The *Wendameen* had taken herself home. As we entered the river, it was as if she saw something familiar, though she had not been there in seventy-two years. Now she was docked less than a half a mile

Our berth in New London from December 1986 till January 1988. It was hard watching the boat deteriorate.

from her original mooring. Recovering some of my senses, I dug deeper through Lloyds and came across names I could not pronounce—Uihlein and L'Amoreaux—then Ford.

I spent the next three weeks in the library reading every microfilm of the *New London Day* from 1900 until 1925. I wanted to find out everything I could about Bliss and the *Wendameen*. I went to other libraries, as well, and I spent a day at the New York Yacht Club going through its records and scrapbooks. Though what I found was interesting, it was of no help. Yet.

That January I got a call from someone on City Island who was interested in buying the masts I had left behind. He told me he knew a fellow by the name of Pfeiffer who used to work on the *Wendameen* and was still living in Port Washington. Within a short time, I was on Paul Pfeiffer's doorstep on a warm winter day. He was in his 80s and hard at work, scraping paint from the windowsills at the front of his house. He invited me in and introduced me to his wife; then we settled down for a long conversation.

He brought out his picture albums, pointed to other photographs on the walls, and shared his stories of the *Wendameen*. She came to life for me for the first time. After that, I never saw her as a rotting hulk again. Paul breathed life into the dying schooner and helped me find her pulse. He told me of L'Amoreaux and how I might find Paul Jr., who would be in his 70s. I spent one more afternoon with Paul Pfeiffer about a week later. He gave me a stack of old negatives and told me of the ship's clock he had engraved for Paul L'Amoreaux and the *Wendameen*, a gift that had since disappeared. I took some pictures on that visit and hoped to see him again.

That didn't happen. I exchanged written greetings with Mr. and Mrs. Pfeiffer for many years but never saw them again.

Meanwhile, I found Paul L'Amoreaux Jr. living just outside of Chicago. We had several great talks over the telephone. He sent me the old family scrapbook to copy. The pages brimmed with old photographs, yellowed newspaper clippings, and stories by Paul L'Amoreaux Sr. and others, pieces that had been published at the time. I pored over every inch looking for information and details.

That whole winter and on into spring I took care of my schooner. During storms I would spend the day and night nearby in my car or on board tending her lines as she pitched about in easterly gales. On good days I would pull the tarps back and try to let her dry out. Several boats on either side of her sank that winter, but the *Wendameen* managed to survive. I researched her history and started to publicize her fate. Joined by a friend who was a professional fundraiser and lobbyist, I approached Connecticut Public Television. They agreed to do a documentary on the schooner if we raised the money—just another $60,000.

At that point I was willing to try anything, make any compromise. I just wanted to see the schooner saved. If that meant living in Connecticut, so be it. But raising the money was impossible. No one believed I could restore the schooner for the $150,000 I thought it would take—not when the big shots we approached for financial help had to spend $40,000 just to have their 50' yachts painted.

By June I was broke. In the course of my life, I have been poor, and I have been really poor. Poor is better. I was down to a tank of gas in the car and enough change for the tolls to Maine when I took a job in Rockland as the captain of a Friendship sloop. I tried not to feel anything as I drove away from the *Wendameen* and left her in the care of a friend.

I spent part of that summer sailing, but mostly I wrote letters, sent out

The starboard side of the saloon. Sunlight pours in from the gap where the deck should be.

press releases, and tried to stay focused on one thing—bringing my boat to Maine. When August ended, I went to Portland to captain the schooner *Sylvina W. Beal* for a couple of months, all the while hoping to get a break on the *Wendameen*. I saw her only once that season, and she looked awful.

In the fall of 1987, almost a year after buying the schooner, I received word that the New London dock she was tied to was about to be torn down. The *Wendameen* had to be moved or become landfill. I was just starting to catch up on the bills from the previous winter. There was no way to move her nor any place to take her. Then the September issue of *Yachting* magazine came out with a small story and picture illustrating the schooner's plight. Days later I received a message to get in touch with an Amory Carhart—the grandson of Chester W. Bliss!

After a phone conversation, I mailed Amory a letter and photos explaining the *Wendameen*'s current state. By mid-October Mr. Carhart sent me a generous check with the note, "Lots of luck with the old girl." Again I tried to get her to Maine. A local man who ran tours on his lobster boat offered to go get the schooner with me. After jury-rigging his boat with a spare fuel tank on deck, we set out in late November.

We were not long underway when he stopped to pour eight quarts of oil into the engine and announced that we would duck into Friendship for a couple of extra cases. All loaded up, we headed offshore, pouring oil into the crankcase at an alarming rate. The seas were rough, the forecast was worse, and I was tired and getting a bit ill. I don't remember which side of Monhegan we were on when I yelled above the noise of the engine, "Let's turn around!" Nightfall brought with it a storm that certainly would have ended any concerns I had in this world.

In early January, under the loom of a wrecking ball, the *Wendameen* was moved in the nick of time. I was not aboard her for her tow to Westbrook, Connecticut. She was in good hands, and I stayed in Maine trying to keep travel to an affordable minimum. Money was tight. I found a small apartment in Rockport, under the home of a local sailmaker. My front door was barely passable because I had stacked the front yard and the apartment with all the *Wendameen* gear from Gerald Ford's house. Lucky for me, my landlords liked boats.

I had to sell some items from time to time, but nothing that would be needed for the restoration. One day, while on errands in Portland, I saw a small gramophone in a junk shop. Even though it was not the same as the one in Paul Pfeiffer's photographs, it was cheap and it worked. At the time my average bank balance was $250, and I talked myself out of buying it. A month later the gramaphone was still there, and I knew the Wendy should have it.

About two weeks after she was towed, I went down to see the *Wendameen*'s new berth. One of the other Maine schooner captains, a good friend, went with me. Captain Ed Glaser was one of the few who encouraged me.

The *Wendameen* was tied up at Pilots Point Marina, which was managed by a very sympathetic Reeves Potts. At the time there was still a chance that the money might be raised to restore her in Connecticut. Potts hauled the schooner out of the water for the cameras then launched her the next day. I did not rush home to wait for the phone to ring. Things were bleak. I picked up a bit of short-term work here and there, but would not commit to anything long term. I felt relief must be just around the corner.

That break finally came in April 1988, when I received a call from an older gentleman who had seen an article about my schooner. His uncles, Robert and Erwin Uihlein, used to own the *Wendameen*. He would be in Maine on business, and he invited me to dinner. A few weeks later, I met Mr. Robert Brumder at the hotel where he and his wife were staying. He brought pictures he had from a 1916 cruise out of Milwaukee. I looked at one photo and was amazed to see a gramophone identical to the one I had just purchased. Mr. Brumder told stories of the *Wendameen*, but really he was sharing his uncle's tales. He hadn't been born yet.

His father had died when he was very young, and his uncles had raised him like a son. Mr. Brumder grew up getting to know his father through their eyes. They had pictures of his older brother, who was aboard the schooner on many occasions. Brumder himself thought he might have sailed on the *Wendemeen* when his mother was pregnant with him. Before dinner, he told his story; after dinner, he wanted to hear mine. I told him of the other boats I had captained, of the difficulties of trying to get the *Wendameen* to Maine. He was concerned for the schooner's future and understood that Maine was the best place for her. He wanted to know what it would take to save her.

I told him that $5,000 would buy a used engine and propeller, fix the rudder, and put some fuel aboard. Once in Maine, the rest would fall into place. We spoke forever of things in general; all the while his wife listened quietly, asking a question here and there. The evening done, we shook hands as Mr. Brumder promised to send copies of his photographs. That feast was the first time in a month I had not eaten frozen pizza. A week later I received a call from a Mr. So-and-So: "Hello, I am calling for Mr. Robert Brumder. He wishes to wire you $5,000. What is your account number?"

Neal Parker

The long shot

I remember my mother in Brooklyn telling her friends, "I wish we had encouraged Neal to become an actor. . . . He couldn't be worse off than he is now, and at least he'd have a job as a waiter."

It was early summer, and Reeves Potts and the crew at Pilots Point Marina were starting to realize that there was no money to restore the *Wendameen* in Connecticut. She was taking up prime dock space and beginning to cost them money. When I presented my plan, Reeves couldn't have been more relieved or helpful. I brought the boatyard the two halves of the *Wendameen*'s rudder, which they patched together. Then they hauled the schooner, stuck in a used engine, and found a respectable used propeller. In general they made sure that the equipment would last long enough to get the *Wendameen* clear of their docks and past the channel, so that if she sank she would not block summer traffic. In fact, they did a decent job of the installation.

It was July 27 when my crew and I showed up in Westbrook. With me were the dauntless Sam Kirby and Tim Coffrin. Sam was an old sailing friend from the *Mamie A. Mister* days. He had thousands of miles of sea experience and was always good company. Tim, a Vietnam vet, survival instructor, musician, and world-class storyteller, had sailed with me as crew on some more recent adventures. Both were valiant souls.

We are entering the choppy waters of the Race, a tide rip by the east end of Long Island Sound. I don't know if our little sail did much, but it made me feel better.

The *Wendameen* at anchor. The first night on our trip we tucked behind the breakwater in Pt. Judith Rhode Island.

We loaded the schooner with food, water, and other supplies for our journey. By evening we had rigged a small mast and sail. I was not about to rely entirely on an engine. Another reason for the mast was to give us some rigging to hold onto when we needed to "go to the head." (Statistically, when a man is lost at sea and the body is found, more often than not his fly is open.) My folks came to see the schooner that evening for the first time. It would take a separate book to describe their reaction. They took us out for a last hot meal.

Sam and I laid some old plywood in the cockpit to keep us from falling through while Tim rigged an awning using some old oars and line. We slept well. The next morning we made a final check of the engine, fuel, pumps, radio, and other equipment. Just before getting underway, the *Wendameen* crew joined the Pilot's Point crew at their coffee break. One of them called across the table, "What's the second oldest Alden schooner?"

I didn't know and asked, "Why?"

He answered, "I want to buy it, because by tonight it will be the oldest."

It was a classic July morning—the sky powder blue, the air hazy and calm. As we cast off, the world beyond the *Wendameen* disappeared. Just a nudge of the throttle and she took off like a swan, with barely a ripple to her wake. The wind came onshore in the afternoon, which was handy because the engine began to overheat, and we had to set our small sail for a while. In short order, however, the engine was back up and running. By the end of the day we had left Connecticut below the horizon. We had gotten underway at 11 A.M. and anchored in Point Judith, Rhode Island, six hours later. By that time we were almost deaf from the engine noise. The exhaust came straight up through the hatch in a pipe without a muffler, passing just three feet from the makeshift tiller.

The second day started wet and foggy. We did not have any navigation equipment except for a misguided old dory compass, which we had to correct by moving canned peaches around it. That night we anchored in Onset, Massachusetts, near the entrance to the Cape Cod Canal. Two locals set out from shore to visit the strange sight in their harbor. After we gave them a tour of the *Wendameen*, they rowed away and returned about an hour later with 4' of stovepipe to help get the exhaust above our faces. Thank you gentlemen, wherever you are! We crawled under Tim's cockpit awning, told stories, and called it a night. By morning we had found out just how much the awning leaked.

We were underway by 6:30. It was flat calm. We passed through the canal and headed north to Gloucester. By mid-afternoon we were dockside, putting another 50 gallons of fuel in the blue plastic drums that made up our tanks. We

July 27, 1988. We are headed home to Maine, and Sam Kirby takes the helm. The makeshift exhaust pipe is coming up through the old engine-room hatch.

Tim demonstrates his survival skills with nothing but a large knife and a watermelon.

Tim takes bow watch in the clearing fog. We are by Thatcher's Island, near Gloucester, Massachusetts.

Tim (left) and I at the helm somewhere off Portland, Maine, on day five of the *Wendameen*'s trip home

Another shot of the fifth day. In the last few miles before Camden the fog finally eased up. Sam stands to the left, while I take the helm.

anchored in the inner harbor for the night. The fishing fleet lined the shore around us. We watched as it told an ageless story.

At 7 A.M. we moved into the outer harbor, but the fog was so thick that I decided we should anchor again. By 9 A.M. we could see almost half a mile. There was no wind, and the tide was in our favor, so we fisted up the anchor again and headed around Cape Ann. The day continued to clear, and two hours before dark we anchored in Portland, Maine.

The fifth day was a bit nasty, but the last leg was upon us. Underway at 6 A.M. in a heavy swell from the southeast, we took turns hugging the exhaust pipe for warmth. It was raining, with the visibility down to one and a half miles. By the time we were near Seguin Island, off the mouth of the Kennebec River, we could barely see past the bow. We picked our way slowly along the coast. At one point we loomed past a small anchored boat with three men fishing. They almost dropped their rods when they saw us. As we slid past, we could tell that they thought they had seen a ghost. We jumped up and down and yelled, "Americay?" The fog remained thick most of the day. To keep our compass true we could not eat the canned peaches. Finally, ten miles short of Camden, by Owls Head, the sky cleared.

The *Wendameen* was in Penobscot Bay at last.

As we entered Camden I didn't want to go straight to our mooring. Instead we took a victory lap through the inner harbor. As we motored our wreck through the million-dollar yachts, with our exhaust belching and plywood patches everywhere, we attracted more than a few horrified glances from the crowds on shore. I suppose some curiosity was understandable. What we didn't know was that we had come in at the end of a big race, and the crowd was waiting to see a boat that had been dismasted. Tim, Sam, and I were very pleased with ourselves as we went out, picked up our mooring, and ended our 350-mile adventure.

Neal Parker

The long shot, continued

About a week after our triumphant arrival in Camden, the harbormaster tried to arrest the schooner, and I received word that town officials were quite concerned by the eyesore I had placed at the entrance to their otherwise perfect harbor. But by this point, I didn't care what people thought; I had to get the project underway.

That involved raising more money and finding a place to haul the schooner. No regular boatyard wanted to risk getting stuck with a rotten old hulk. Still, over the next two months I managed to get the ball rolling. A local businessman who owned the neighborhood movie house made me a generous open-ended loan, and Mr. Carhart sent another check. Several friends who were boatbuilders offered to get involved, but I didn't want them to risk tying up their small savings for an uncertain period of time.

I kept sending out press releases, and the *Wendameen* got some favorable publicity. But raising money was slow going. People told me get a job at one of the local yards, but I never knew anyone who could salt away $150,000 quickly at $8 an hour. I tried all the local banks, but the answer was always the same: "No."

October arrived, and the smell of autumn gales was in the air. With an-

This item appeared in the *Portland Press Herald* of September 27, 1988. Our arrival in Camden fostered some news coverage. The town fathers were in an uproar over the wreck I had placed in their harbor. Others who were more understanding, would row out to the old hull and watch the sunset through her sides.

Grand old schooner faces dubious future

Courtesy of Sandra Haimila

Hauling out in Rockland. It took three cranes and nine hours to lift the schooner and move her just two hundred feet.

other $5,000 from Mr. Brumder and about the same from other sources, I was finally able to haul the *Wendameen* and buy some lumber. With the help of Captain Ed Glaser, we moved the schooner down to Rockland, where I hired two large cranes to pick her up and set her on the seawall at Prock Marine, a local dock-building company. Two hours into the first attempt, they almost toppled their cranes under the weight of the waterlogged hull. The crane operators had to let the *Wendameen* fall to keep themselves from going over. My heart jumped as the old hull dropped about ten feet onto the hard mud bottom. I thought she would split in two.

The two operators wanted to give up, but I insisted on their getting a third crane. We waited an hour before it joined us, but finally—with two cranes lifting the stern and one raising the bow—the *Wendameen* cleared the water and was set on dry land. The whole business took about nine hours to complete. That night, a bad easterly came up the coast, a storm that would have finished the *Wendameen* had she been on her mooring.

I had told a lot of people that I was going to restore the schooner; I had to do it or no one would ever take me at my word again.

The first step was to carefully remove what was left of the *Wendameen*'s interior. When I bought the schooner two years earlier I was prepared to modify her to look more like the working boats I had grown up on. I even thought of changing her name, since no one could pronounce it anyway. But over time she had shown me who she was and had revealed her past. Now, as I picked up tools for the first time, I was determined to make the Wendy her old self again. As I began to take her apart, I stopped and worshiped every original pencil line

Fred off to port with a large wrecking tool. We gutted the schooner bit by bit so that we could get at the frames from inside. The 30'-long cabin top was barely suspended.

and preserved every screw I found in the cupboards, lockers, and bulkheads. I carefully cut each nail by hand, removing panels one piece at a time, studying and numbering every part as I went.

All the while, the hull was caving in around me.

One day big, burly Fred, whom I knew from the waterfront, came down. He was out of work and offered his services. I hired him for the day. We worked together for an hour or so taking the interior apart, when I announced I had to run some errands. I told Fred to keep at his project and said the chainsaw was handy if one of the bigger timbers was in the way. When I came back, the chainsaw smoke had yet to clear the air, and the whole of the *Wendameen*'s interior was lying in a heap in the bilge.

Fred looked pleased as I stared in disbelief. I grabbed his hand and, shaking it, I said, "Thank you Fred, I couldn't have done that myself!" Things went a little more quickly after that. With the help of a fifteen-year-old high-school student named Tom Lokocz, I proceeded to try to straighten out the shape of the sagging hull. Tom had been my deckhand the previous summer on the Friendship sloop *Irene.* He was an eager wharf rat and, though young, was smart enough to volunteer his labor only until he was too valuable to lose.

The schooner's sides were completely rotten and had actually begun to cave in. With the interior removed, Tom and I spread the topsides apart sixteen inches before the *Wendameen* began to look right. The stern had dropped down about eight inches, so we jacked and posted it.

Through most of that first winter, I worked seven days a week, primarily alone, replacing the majority of the schooner's frames. The weather was cold, and from time to time I ran the chainsaw exhaust against my hands just to get some feeling back in my fingers. Tom rode his bicycle down on weekends, and I paid him what I could. Fred would show up from time to time and tear something apart. His wife would on occasion make sandwiches for both of us. When I ran out of money in February, I sold my truck to buy lumber. Fred kept working when he could, taking in trade a small wooden sailboat that I had planned to fix up.

I kept visiting the local banks and, instead of asking for money, I just kept them apprised of my progress. With a survey in hand, I showed them what I was doing, what the schooner would be worth in a month when I spent such and such. Every thirty days I went back with a fresh survey and showed them I was meeting my goals. By early March, the framing was almost done, but I was broke again.

Mr. Brumder offered to come through once more but only if I could find another source of funds, as well. I went back to the banks with a simple proposal. I needed $40,000 to finish the *Wendameen*'s hull and get her back in the water. I offered to put $10,000 in escrow if they would lend me $30,000—assuming I had enough equity in the schooner after "borrowing" my $10,000. Lucky for me it was 1989, and the banks were very liberal. Finally, one of them agreed to my plan.

In April I hired a real boatbuilder, James Parker (no relation). I had finished replacing about 75 percent of the *Wendameen*'s frames, and now, working with Jim, I began to replace her planking. Watching every penny, I built staging out of the scraps I had from the framing stock. Later, when the staging came down, the wood was used again for the boat's new interior.

I became Jim's helper. I would show up at the schooner at about 6:30 A.M., get out the tools, and cut away the bad planks we had discussed replacing the previous day. We would work until about 4 P.M. When he left I'd take an hour to clean up and then go home. Some days we would hang and fasten three planks; on other days we'd replace one or none, depending on what additional problems were found. The schedule was grueling, but surveys satisfied the bank, and it loaned me money over and above what I had placed in escrow. By late spring, progress was starting to show.

Winter arrived, and work proceeded under cover. There was no heat, no shop—just a cold, empty schooner. I would often run the hot exhaust from the chainsaw against my hands as the only way to get the feeling back into my fingers. I was lucky and do not recommend trying this. Working pretty much alone during this time, I had replaced my hired help with a sawhorse. The tarp nailed under the stern covered the bandsaw and a small work space. The trunk of my '66 Plymouth Fury housed my other tools.

Summer arrived. It was torture to look out at the cool waters of Penobscot Bay. The afternoon breeze kept things on shore pleasant enough, but I wanted to go sailing. One Friday afternoon in early July, I tried desperately not to look up from my work to watch the annual schooner race taking place beyond the breakwater. I just kept saying under my breath, "Next year little schooner, next year."

A friend gave me an old dory that had been serving as a flower planter in her yard. Now it was too far gone for even that service. Tom and I hauled it back to the *Wendameen* and, using scraps of lumber and a whole lot of goop, we gave it back some life. With a simple mast, a crude rudder, and a sail made from an old blue tarp, we threw the dory into Camden Harbor. She sailed as expected and after a couple of afternoon jaunts, I hung a "For Sale" sign in the rigging. A week later a tourist from Connecticut bought the boat for $300.

The *Wendameen* was still a big empty shell. But I hired other people on occasion, and work proceeded nicely. At summer's end, with the hull almost done, the bank released my original $10,000, and I went all out to see that the *Wendameen* was ready to launch before fall. Jim and I worked on framing the deck, while two caulkers made the seams tight with cotton and oakum. One of them was the son of the man who had caulked the *Wendameen* at Nevins Shipyard back in 1936. He had gone into his father's trade and had even done some work on the schooner for Mr. Ford. Semi-retired, he was now living in Maine.

A report from the *Courier-Gazette,* in Rockland, on March 21, 1989. Working mostly alone, I took about four months to complete the framing.

FRAMING OUT — Neal Parker stands next to Wendameen's port frames and explains how he is replacing the old, rotted ones with locally grown hackmatack.

Staff Photo by Steve Heddericg

Yacht Restoration One-Man Job

November 6, 1989, was launching day. The *Wendameen* was just a bare hull. There was still no decking, but the beams were in.

In September we had a huge putty-and-paint party, and the old *Wendameen* started to shine. During the previous summer, I had met Reuel Parker (again, no relation), a most unusual naval architect and boatbuilder from Florida. We became good friends. He was enthused by the *Wendameen*'s restoration and offered much valuable advice. With the hull nearing completion, he took it upon himself to help redesign the vessel's interior plan to accommodate the needs of the charter business.

I wanted to launch the schooner at this point because she was fairly light. Every day that we added timber was a day she might become too heavy to launch from our makeshift shipyard. On November 6, 1989, the cranes came back and easily put the *Wendameen* overboard. Though just half finished, she looked impressive. After the small crowd left, Jim Parker and I stood on the dock looking quietly at our handiwork. During our six months together, I had come to realize that Jim's idea of a compliment upon seeing something I had worked on was, "I've seen worse."

With a tired stare, I broke the momentary silence and said, "Well, Jim . . . what do we do now?"

In his classic mutter he said, "I don't know. . . by now anybody I ever worked for had run out of money." He was right of course. It was time for another trip to the bank.

Carl once taught me, "If you owe the bank $10,000 you have a problem. If you owe the bank $20,000 dollars you have real problems, but if you owe the bank $40,000 dollars, *they* have problems." I was counting on that. Now my offer to the bank was simple: If you ever want to see your money again, I need $100,000 to finish the schooner. Carl was right again. If I watched every penny, it looked as if we might just pull this off.

Initially I had hoped to keep the *Wendameen* in the water once the hull was finished because this would save money. Jim, however, quickly talked me out of it. The railway at the North End Shipyard, where I had apprenticed twelve years before, was available for the winter, and we would only have to move the schooner several hundred yards.

Once she was hauled, we built a rickety cover over her, and I started to hire some crew. It was, I think, the coldest December on record. The tempera-

Reuel Parker showed up from Florida in the nick of time with his portable shipyard. It looked like a giant hot-dog stand filled with power tools. He worked miracles, building a total of seven cabin doors, six locker doors, and much of the interior trim in less than a week, using scraps from the lumber pile.

ture never got above nine degrees. By January there were about three full-timers besides me working on board. I spent most of my time on the interior while others did decks and rails. By February, Jim was cursing every penny I tried to save, and I was starting to feel like the errand boy. I continued to work weekends when no one was around, but when the full gang was at the shipyard, they kept sending me for bolts, lumber, saw blades, putty, and—of course—coffee. I was also starting to get caught up in the litany of paperwork involved in Coast Guard licensing, bank loans, and press releases needed to get a business started. Still I managed to put in a full forty hours a week directly on board.

Winter was about to end, and I knew I had to get serious about a few other details like masts and sails. I had none. I hoped to find trees big enough to make solid masts. The foremast would be only 56' long. The mainmast was the problem. Finished, it would measure 75' with a diameter of 11". Every log I looked at came up short, so I was finally forced to look into gluing up the mast. This ended up being the budget buster, but I resolved to do it rather than shorten the *Wendameen*'s rig.

I found some used sails that my landlords, the sailmakers, were kind enough to alter. Our 1,200-square-foot main was a twenty-five-year-old canvas sail from the larger charter schooner *Timberwind*. It fit like a glove. We made a foresail out of a thirty-year-old main from a smaller schooner. The jib was cut from a yacht's retired genoa, and the staysail was one of the forty-year-old sails I had obtained from Mr. Ford. They would have to do.

Another difficulty was coming up with five tons of ballast to put in the hull. Lead pre-cast into twenty-pound pigs was selling for close to ninety cents a pound. I did not have $10,000 to spend on ballast. I considered railroad track and steel ball bearings mixed with cement. I even contacted the local nuclear power plant to see if they had anything heavy lying around. At last I found a scrap dealer who had five tons of lead in the form of old wire sheathing. It cost ten cents a pound.

One of my crew spent a week alongside the *Wendameen* melting down the metal and ladling it into bread pans. Once cooled, the roughly cast pigs were dumped out and the pans refilled. Each pig weighed about thirty-five pounds. It then took half a day for ten people to pass them hand-to-hand up into the schooner and down to me. I then placed them in the vessel's bilge.

Spring had come, and the shipyard needed the railway for the rest of the schooner fleet, so on April 8, 1990, we launched the still partially finished *Wendameen*. It was a cold and drizzly morning when she slid back into the harbor. A crowd had gathered to watch this more dignified launching. By now the naysayers had started to realize that I would get the job done.

I hoped we might be sailing by June and had actually taken a couple of passenger reservations for that month. However the work from here on seemed to take twice as long as I had anticipated. We were dealing with plumbing and electrical systems, mast-making, blacksmithing, and thousands of small details that slowed the more obvious work. Young Tom, who had earned the job as mate for the coming summer, continued to show up after school and on weekends. He worked on paint and varnish, while some of the carpenters built the rails, and Jim built the cockpit.

We were in the water, dockside, and trying not to trip over each other as the *Wendameen* seemed to get smaller. By early June the masts were in, and Tom and I worked on the rigging and sails as fresh wood shavings blew all around us. My friend Reuel Parker had returned from Florida in time to build doors and interior trim. Then, suddenly, I was out of money again. I went back to the bank and asked for just $3,000 to get us up and running. They said no. Three of the carpenters said goodbye. Some took my tools in trade for pay.

Jim, Reuel, and Tom stayed on. They wanted to see the *Wendameen* sailing. Captain Ed came to visit. He and the owners of North End Shipyard were aware of my dilemma. They offered to loan me what I needed as soon as their seasons were underway and as cash flow allowed. I was dumbstruck at this generosity, and after the offer sank in I said that I hoped the loan would not be needed.

We now redoubled our efforts. I think we were working at least ten hours a day and getting very tired. On July 1 at 2 P.M., there were seven people on the dock waiting for their cruise. As the vacationers stood looking down at the *Wendameen*, they must have been startled by what they saw. Tom was cramming the new mattresses down the hatch as I ripped the packaging off the pillows and linens, which I had purchased with my newly acquired credit card. Several friends were sweeping sawdust from the deck, and another was loading groceries for that night's supper.

I explained to my guests that there would be a slight delay as we were just about to "finish the schooner's restoration." I added, "After I show you your cabins, could you please stay out of them until evening as the paint is still a bit wet?" Finally, at 3 P.M., I started the engine. There was no chance for a shakedown cruise, but I felt confident and ready to go. Our sixteen-year-old mate cast off the lines, and I put the engine in forward.

The gearshift lever came apart in my hand. It was time to hoist sail.

We later experienced some minor difficulties, such as the water system bursting into the partially cooked bread. But as a whole, things went smoothly. That night we had beef stew and brownies. As I sat in my rocking chair looking forward, I never knew that food could taste so good.

The view aft along the port side. Some of the bad frames are visible in the foreground. The main companionway is marked by its ladder, leaning off to the side.

Finally work begins. I had waited two years for this day. My first official act was to hit my thumb with a twelve-pound sledge hammer. Here we are looking forward on the starboard side. The curved cockpit coaming is in the foreground. Farther along, where the deck beams are missing, are the timbers that we used to stretch the hull back to her original shape.

New frames going into the port side. As I made them up, I only secured the hull planks that I planned to keep. When the framing was done I figured most of the bad planking would just fall out. By the time I had my method down pat, I could make patterns for a frame from keel to deck, remove the bad timber, cut the new one, and have it bolted in place in about eight hours. When I had help, the job took seven hours.

The interior has been removed, and we are looking forward along the keel. The foredeck and beams are still intact and were left in place temporarily to keep the weakened hull together. The long, sweeping timbers are called bilge stringers. They add to the hull's longitudinal strength. Eventually they, too, were replaced.

A RESTORATION ALBUM

In April 1989, I was finally able to hire a real boat builder, Jim Parker. I became his assistant. I never removed more planking than could be replaced in a day. It's too easy to get ahead of yourself.

Jim, left, drills holes while I pound spikes. By this time I had been working ten hours a day, seven days a week. I showed up an hour before Jim to set up tools and tear out planks. After he left for the day, I would spend an hour or so packing up tools and gazing at the schooner.

This is the port side, where the cockpit should be. I had replaced about 60 percent of the *Wendameen's* frames on each side of the keel. Here, the long trunk cabin still hangs on. It took me a long time to part with it emotionally. Finally we salvaged the skylights and hatches, and carefully cut up the cabin into manageable pieces.

Planks marked for removal. The shortest we put in was about 12' long. The longest was about 30' long. One of the original planks from 1912 ran from the stem almost to the stern. It measured 55' long.

Summer continues. Here you are looking at the new planking on the starboard side.

I take a break by the bandsaw. Above me the hull has been faired, sanded, and primed. The transom still needs to be replaced. Other than that, there was no tearing out left to do. We put in new wood from this point on.

Two days before we launched, I realized we had nothing on the schooner to tie to. Jim, seen here, hurriedly installed a new pawl post while I put new bits in the stern.

Looking aft at the new sheer clamp, beam shelf, and deck beams. The old *Wendameen* gets stronger by the day. The original pawl post is still standing. It would take a small gang to sway the iron windlass off its base, so I put that off as long as possible.

This item appeared in the *Camden Herald*. It was frightening to watch the hull swing around in the air like a drunken marionette.

SCHOONER LAUNCHING: After a year of reframing, redecking and replanking, the schooner *Wendameen* was launched in Rockland Harbor Monday afternoon. The job was performed by two cranes, as dozens of spectators and volunteers watched from parked vehicles, sheltered from the rain. Ship owner Neal Parker, of Rockport, says only 20 percent of the 67-foot-long vessel will be original when the restoration is completed, and she still needs a lot of work before she actually sails. Thomas Mark Szelog

The work continues, now at North End Shipyard. That December the temperature never got above nine degrees. Tim, seen here bundled up, came to help with the interior. He crouches where the galley will soon be. Bottom center we see the keel with the new mainmast step.

Jim stands in the "cockpit" and measures the deck for a second layer of plywood. I'm standing in the background, where the main hatch will go. The bulkheads (partitions) behind me were my project at the time.

Late January. The deck is now on. Two layers of plywood and fiberglass ensure that there will never be a leaky bunk. Jim lays out a 30'-long pine timber that will make up the starboard cabin side.

Late April. Standing on the heel of the mainmast, one of the crew shapes the spar by hand.

Looking toward the horizon. The *Wendameen*'s long rest is almost over.

Arrangement of the stern and main sheet.

The saloon gets some paint.

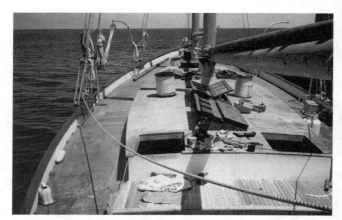

Looking down the port side. It is mid-June and I just ran out of money. The skylights are in place and the hatches are cut. Work progresses on the cockpit.

The cockpit seemed to take forever. Jim kept getting pulled away from working on it to help with other jobs.

It is 1 P.M. In a few minutes our first guests would arrive. Several friends help put the mattresses below.

We're finally underway.

Under sail during the Great Schooner Race of 1990.This report appeared in the *Camden Herald* of July 12:

" . . . Probably most notable was the performance of the *Wendameen,* since this is the first time she has raced in 57 years. Even without topsails, she was a formidable match for many of the larger boats in her windward class. At the start of the race, she had the unfortunate position of being the leeward vessel, so Captain Neal Parker took an early tack soon after all engines were cut at Fiddler's Ledge. Although he lost ground with this maneuver, he was confident that his newly restored 67' passenger vessel would do well.

"And, she did indeed, passing first one, then another, and yet another of the larger vessels carrying hundreds more square feet of sail. It was truly thrilling, and sincere shouts of approval and applause came from many of the other schooners.The passengers were excited by the yacht's performance and the perfect sailing conditions.

"In fact, at the end of the day, several of them were already signed up for next year's Great Schooner Race aboard the *Wendameen.*"

Epilogue

When we set sail that July, the *Wendameen* was not quite finished. Over the next three months, each time we came dockside, either Reuel or Jim would meet us and add some trim, finish a rail, or fit a hatch cover. Then Tom would sweep the deck and we'd go sailing again.

In the middle of the summer a small package arrived from Chester Bliss's grandson Amory Carhart. Enclosed were the *Wendameen*'s engraved silver lobster forks, the ones that were on board for her original launching in 1912. Amory's kind note said he was pleased to see them returned home.

Since then, other Bliss grandchildren—and great grandchildren—have come aboard. There is even an Addison among them. Mr. Brumder and his family sailed with us the first two summers, and a couple of his grandchildren come out on a regular basis. Paul L'Amoreaux's grandson came to visit one fall. His face was compellingly like his grandfather's, which I had come to know so well while poring over the old photographs for so many years. Later, he generously sent along many of his family's *Wendameen* keepsakes, knowing that they would have a good home.

To this day, the restoration continues in small ways, but now that work is combined with months of upkeep and maintenance. At first, I was disappointed that we had to replace so much of the *Wendameen*. She looked so new, and much of her patina had been lost. Now, however, we are about to enter our twelfth year of sailing together, and she is developing that wear and softness around the edges that only time brings. The *Wendameen* has proven herself to be a survivor while adding new history to an already illustrious past. She has also found a home here in Maine with schooners that are her contemporaries in time and significance.

I have come to realize that I am passing through her life and not the opposite. I hope that in fifty years the *Wendameen*'s captain cares as much about her as I do and perhaps tells his guests of "some guy in the last century who pulled her off a mud bank."

In 1992 the Wendameen *was placed on The National Register of Historic Places.*

That's me at the helm. I was told to include this picture. . . .

Sailing like the ghost she almost was . . .

The *Wendameen* is in good company. Here she fights to pass the *American Eagle* to windward on Penobscot Bay. The *Eagle* was a working fisherman. John Alden would be pleased.

We sail her hard, and she earns her keep.

Appendix

The following information was furnished by the John G. Alden Company.

The original typed specifications, reproduced here, describe in detail the materials and methods to be used in the construction of Design No. 21 (not yet named the *Wendameen*). They accompanied the blueprints that were sent to various shipyards for bids on building the schooner. The contract eventually went to the Frank Adams Shipyard in East Boothbay, Maine.

The date on the lines drawings is December 31, 1911. This means that from the time the design was finished until the *Wendameen* was launched, not much more than five months had elapsed! That's not very long considering there were no power tools and the keel was laid in the dead of a Maine winter. Some changes to the plans and specifications were made during construction. A good naval architect knows how to take advice from a good shipwright.

The lines drawings presented here for study are sized to fit the pages rather than reproduced at any particular scale. For model builders, properly scaled plans can be purchased through John G. Alden, Naval Architects, 89 Commercial Wharf, Boston, MA 02108 telephone (617) 227-9480, aldendesign@att.net.

I have built several models of the *Wendameen* using the company's plans. Careful study of the photographs in this book will serve to fill in the missing details.

SPECIFICATIONS NO. 21, 50 FT. WATERLINE SCHOONER YACHT DESIGNED FOR CHESTER W. BLISS, BY JOHN G. ALDEN.

IN GENERAL:

In carrying out these specifications it is understood that all workmanship shall be first class and materials used shall be of good quality; that the stock shall be reasonably clear and free from all defects; and that the yacht shall be built, fitted and furnished with everything necessary to make her complete and ready for sea, with the exception of nautical instruments, upholstery, linen, dishes, boatswain's stores, and similar portable outfit and with any other exceptions mentioned below. The specifications and drawings are intended to co-operate so that any works exhibited in the drawings and not mentioned in these specifications, or vice-versa, are to be executed the same as if they were mentioned in the specifications and set forth in the drawings without any extra charge whatever.

No changes to be made in either the plans or specifications without the written consent of the Architect.

DIMENSIONS

Length overall: 67' 0"
Length on waterline: 50' 7"
Beam extreme: 17' 0"
Draught: 8' 8"

WOOD KEEL

Maple or Yellow Birch sided 12" amidships and moulded as shown. Siding tapered in ends as shown.

IRON KEEL

Not to weigh less than 7¼ tons and to be secured with fourteen 1¼ galvanized iron bolts set up with nuts and washers on top of keel as shown on plan.

INSIDE BALLAST

To consist of 7¼ tons of lead pigs to be supplied and properly stowed by builder.

STEM

Oak, sided 7" and moulded as per plans, scarphed and bolted to keel with Four ¾" galvanized iron clinch bolts, or screw bolts.

STERN POST

Oak, sided 8" tapered at heel.

DEADWOOD

Of oak or maple, as shown, securely bolted together and to keel with ¾" galvanized iron bolts clinched over malleable washers.

FRAMES

Selected double moulded white oak, spaced 20" on centers, the grain to follow the curvature of frame as far as possible.

Frame timbers sided 2½", moulded 5½" at throats and 4" at heads bolted together with ½" galvanized iron bolts. Chain-plate frames to have butts strapped with galvanized iron with two ⅝" bolts on each side of butt.

FLOORS
All of galvanized wrought iron ¾" × 4" at throats, arms extending 24" clear of keel, one on every frame.

PLANKING
Georgia pine finished thickness 1⅞", fastened with ⅜" × 3½" square galvanized iron ship spikes counterbored and bunged.

No streak to be wider than 6" from lower turn of bilge up. Bottom planks, except three lower, not over 8" wide—6" plank to have two fastenings to a frame. [In the original specifications, the final reference to fastening 8" planks was crossed out by hand.]

CLAMPS
Georgia pine, to be worked in two streaks if necessary, 3" × 10" as shown, tapered at ends to 2½" × 8" extending from stem to quarterlogs, top of clamp to be flush with upper side of deck beams which are to be dovetailed full depth into clamp.

Clamp to be through fastened to sheer strake at every frame with ⁷⁄₁₆" galvanized iron clinch bolts, in addition to the through fastening to shelf.

SHELVES
Of Georgia pine 4" × 5" for ½ length tapered to 3" × 3" at ends, To extend 55' in single lengths and to be through fastened to sheer strake at every frame with ⁷⁄₁₆" galvanized iron clinch bolts, or screw bolts.

BILGE STRINGERS
3" × 8" Georgia pine three on each side tapered at ends, extending as shown on plans. Each stringer to have two through fastenings to each frame.

DECK BEAMS
Oak, spaced generally 20" on centers as shown, crown 6" amidships. Ordinary beams sided 2½", moulded 3½". Partner beams 4" × 4", moulding reduced to 3½ at ends. Beams to be dovetailed into clamp, Beams through screw or clinch bolted to shelf with ⁷⁄₁₆" galvanized iron. Beams finished smooth with lower edges rounded. Chocks 3" × 3" worked between beams under edge of covering board where nec-

essary to make bearing for ends of decking. Foremast partners of 4" white oak with 4" hackmatack double knees at partner.

DECK
Well seasoned white pine in long lengths free from knots, shakes, and sap, dressed 2" × 2", laid fore and aft with edge of grain up and fastened to beams with ⁵⁄₁₆" × 3" round galvanized iron spikes. Ends nibbed into covering board counterbored and plugged.

PLANKSHEER
White oak 2" × 8" mortised over frame heads and in not more than three pieces, with long scarphs, edge bolted, and caulked. Bolted to beams, clamp and sheer strake with ⅜" × 4" galvanized spikes bunged.

SIDE OF HOUSE
Of 1⅞" white oak sprung to shape of planksheer and fitted over 3½" × 3½" oak sill as shown. Corners at ends moulded from 5" × 2" pieces of white oak, to be clinch bolted to sill and two through bolts at each portlight.

HOUSE SILL
White oak 3" × 3½", deck beams to be mortised into sill and tie rods on each side of ½" galvanized iron from sill to sheer strake at each third deck beam.

HOUSE BEAMS
All selected white oak spaced 1' 3" on centers, three at mainmast 3" × 3" as shown, others sided 2" and moulded 3". All dovetailed into side of house.

TOP OF HOUSE
1½" × 4" matched white pine, beaded on lower edges, laid straight fore and aft, and fastened with 3" galvanized boat nails.

To be smoothed and painted one thick coat and covered with No. 8 seamless duck set in crude turpentine and ironed with hot irons.

COCKPIT
Beams 2" × 3" white oak placed as shown, bolted to stringer at sides and fitted with stanchions of same size where practicable.

Floor same as deck. Two 1½" heavy lead pipe scuppers at forward corners flanged to floors and hull, bedded in white lead, securely fastened and made watertight. Outboard ends of scuppers covered by leather flaps backed with copper opening aft. Staving ⅞" x 2" matched mahogany with beveled edges, fastened into grub at bottom and carlin at top and extending to cap of coaming. Wash rail to be of oak ⅞" thick, steamed and bent and planted on top of deck with 1¼" x 4½" mahogany cap rabbeted over coaming and staving.

KNEES

Eight pairs of 2½" hackmatack hanging knees, including two pair of house beams, lodging knees as shown on plan fastened with ½" galvanized iron bolts clinched over rings.

TIE RODS

One ⅞" diameter galvanized iron tie rod forward of foremast connecting mast step and partners, set up with nut and washers on top and bottom of both step and beam. Also check nut on under side of beam. One 1" rod at mainmast inside 1" brass pipe, pipe to have sockets threaded on each end to screw tight to partner and mast step. A " screw bolt connecting sheer strake and house sill at every third beam space.

BULWARKS

Total height 10½". Rail to be mahogany 1⅞" x 5½" oval section, scored on underside to fit over waist ¼".

Waist ⅞" Georgia pine let in ⅜" inside sheer strake, ⅝" shims placed between waist and frame tops extending to within 1" of planksheer.

Sheet brass chafing guards to be worked on rail where anchors are taken aboard and at gangway. Bulwarks to be supported by galvanized iron knees at chainplates on each side about 2" x ¾" in throats, securely fastened to deck and inside of bulwarks.

RUDDER

Stock, white oak 7" diameter tapered to 3" at heel, hung with brass pintle at heel and by two ⁵⁄₁₆" x 4" Tobin bronze straps around stock. Blade of white oak, tapered at after edge to about 1½" thickness. Two galvanized iron straps ⅜" x 4" to be let in flush in rudder, one above and one below propeller space extending on both sides in one piece and through fastened with ½" galvanized bolts clinched in countersunk holes.

BITTS

To receive heel of bowsprit, to be 3½" x 8" oak tapered at bottom, stepped into stem and securely fastened. Oak key fitted through bitts under deck.

DECK JOINER WORK

There will be five skylights, one companionway and two sliding hatches as shown on plans, all to be built of mahogany and to be watertight when closed. Glass in skylights to be heavy corrugated and hinges to be of the McIntyre patent type. Brass guards set in removable frames to be fitted in skylights, also clamp for fastening inside. Forward sash of galley skylight fitted with three brass skylight fasteners well secured.

Companionway to have heavy brass hasps and padlocks. Wheel box of ⅞" mahogany finished flush all over, boards not to be beaded. Box to fit steerer as snugly as possible.

CHAINPLATES

Galvanized steel, 2½" x ½", 3 ft. long fitted on side of frames as shown, fastened to frame with three ¾" galvanized iron screw bolts to each plate.

Ventilating hatch 5" diameter brass, with screw cover and grating, fitted in deck as far aft as practicable.

Stove pipe of galvanized iron of Liverpool Ventilator pattern with galvanized deck flanges and heavy half oval guards to prevent rope catching rim at top. Oak boom crutch fitted same as on fishing schooners, made stationary. Boat hook with galvanized iron end and 10' oak handle. Oak or hackmatack pinrails at masts, oak or locust pins as required. Deck hooks, eyebolts, ringbolts lignum vitae fair leaders, cleats, chocks, cavils, etc. as required.

Ten oval hinged portlights in sides of house and one in forward end, to have finished brass frames and ⅜" plate glass lights, opening to be 5" x 9" in clear for all lights. All to have hinge and screw clamp. Portlight frames let in flush bedded in white lead and the whole made entirely watertight.

DECK FITTINGS

Windlass to be American Ship Windlass Co's. Fig. 555, with wild cat for ⅝" chain, size C. secured to bitts, complete, with chain pipes and covered, hawse pipes to be galvanized iron fitted through rail. Rail to be suitably reinforced in way of hawse pipes. Steering gear to be Loud-Robinson Edson Mfg. Co's. pattern of suitable size for 7" wood rudder stock complete with mahogany wheel 36" diameter.

A 4" galvanized sheet iron low cowl ventilator fitted with screwplate and solid cover to be placed on house at forward end of engine room.

Sheet travelers for main and fore sheets of galvanized iron 1" diameter and 18" long, also forestaysail traveler of ¾" diameter by 5' long set up with nuts and washers under deck (or house) beams, fitted with rubber buffers, ends of travelers to have guards of oak securely fastened to deck. Side light boards to be supplied by builder.

POWER INSTALLATION

A 50-65 H.P. Standard engine will be installed by builder as per plan on oak foundation, timbers sided 5" over floors sided 3" and 4" let into each other as shown. After end of stringers secured to frames by galvanized iron braces similar to the iron floors, stringers to be bolted through floors and planking with ¾" galvanized iron bolts set up inside with nuts over washers.

A staybolt will also be placed across forward end of engine running through an oak header as large as can be conveniently used and secured with nuts and washers. Floors will also be securely bolted to frames and from planking. A 120 Gal. 28 oz. copper gasoline tank will occupy entire space under bridge deck as shown to be well riveted and soldered and to have five splash partitions placed fore and aft and well secured. It shall be placed in a galvanized iron tray lined with thin wood 9" high draining overboard through lead scuppers at each end. Tank shall be fitted with 2½" filler plate of approved pattern, ¼" vent piped to top of house and fitted with aircock, and supply taken from each end through ⅜" annealed copper piping with threaded joints well set up and soldered, leading to a common "T" fitting thence to carbureter or auxiliary tank. A globe valve shall be fitted on each branch as near the tank as conveniently accessible. Exhaust pipe will be well lined with asbestos to point where overflow water pipe enters. Muffler to be placed at one side of cockpit with exhaust outlet under stern as high up as practicable. A heavy copper drip pan shall be fitted under engine to catch all drip from engine and draining into well at after end. Stern bearing and inside stuffing box to be threaded on stern tube at each end and well fitted and lagbolted to prevent turning. Means for operating reverse gear and controlling engine from the cockpit shall be provided by owner and installed by builder.

ELECTRIC LIGHTING

Wiring shall be provided and placed by builder for sixteen fixtures and to be covered by mahogany moulding. All electrical equipment will be supplied by owner.

INSIDE JOINER WORK

Forecastle to be finished in varnished cypress with table hinged to after partition, three pipe berths and separate toilet room. Iron ladder to forward hatch. Crew's toilet fitted with Sands Fig. S-31 A closet and Sands Plate S-180 tilting basin over closet.

Galley to be finished similar to forecastle and fitted with ice box, sink, dresser, dish locker, shelves, No. 5 Shipmate Range, etc. Space back of range fitted for holding pots, pans etc. Coal hatch placed under floor. Ice chest to have a complete double wall of ⅞" cypress with 2" space between. To be divided into top and bottom compartments as indicated with free communication between compartments at one end. Top compartment for ice, with solid rail about 8" high at the open end. Portable shelves to be arranged as directed.

Engine room to be finished in same manner as galley, fitted with work bench, two fixed bunks, clothes closets and lockers. A locker shall be fitted up under work bench lined with zinc and soldered to make tight joints, to be used for storage of oils. Provision shall also be made under work bench for secure accommodation of lighting storage batteries. Iron ladder to lead to companionway.

Staterooms, saloon and passageways to be finished in white pine painted white. Bureau tops, rails, front of transoms, alcove posts and trimmings, companion steps and base boards to be of mahogany finished bright. Two mirrors to be fitted at forward ends of saloon in place of panels as shown.

Owner's stateroom to have berth 7' × 3' 6", a full length wardrobe, a bureau fitted with three drawers and mirror over and a seat as shown, berth to be also fitted with drawers under. Other stateroom to be arranged similarly with hanging space instead of wardrobe, and berth 6' 4" × 2' 4". Toilet rooms fitted with Sands closets Plate S-28 and Sand's lavatories Plate S-209. Saloon to have two sideboards, alcoves and lockers as shown, transom tops to be hinged at backs and arranged to pull out 12" to form extension. No table is required in saloon.

Partitions: The entire partition around engine room and at aft end of galley is to be made sound and gas proof, and shall be built of ¾" cypress sheathing on inside, then a thickness of felt board, and then paneled on side of saloon and passageway and sheathed on after end, special care being taken to insure good fitting at corners and where partition joins hull.

Floor throughout to be matched rift hard pine in 3" uniform widths laid close and blind fastened on beams of 2" × 3" spruce spaced 20". Hatches to be fitted in floor as follows: Two in galley about 18" square, a long hatch on each side of cabin 15" × 12", each in 6' sections. All to be substantially constructed with hardwood cleats on lower side at close intervals. Allowance to be made for swelling.

All shelves to have rails about 2½" high. Transoms in forecastle to have ⅞" smooth cypress tops and matched fronts, tops to have hatches for access to space below.

CEILING

To be worked back of all seats, berths and lockers, ¾" × 3" matched cypress or pine.

INSIDE PAINTING & VARNISHING

To be first class in every respect and satisfactory to Architect. No enamel paint to be used. Color scheme to be as directed by Architect or Owner. Paint to be pure white lead, linseed oil and turpentine, with only the addition of the necessary coloring. Varnish to be first quality interior varnish.

Base boards, top of wash stand, bureau, cabin stairs, all mahogany parts in saloon and stateroom and entire galley, engine room, and forecastle to be varnished. The rest of cabin painted a sufficient number of coats to make a smooth and workmanlike finish.

All work to be rubbed sufficiently to secure a smooth and uniform finish.

HARDWARE FITTINGS

All hinges to be cast brass with brass pins. Locks to be of brass or bronze and of approved make, pressed glass knobs to be used on doors in owner's stateroom, drop rings on passageway side of other doors, closet door catches in saloon, staterooms, and toilets to be cast bronze with "T" or oval handles. A mahogany hand rail with brass stanchions to be fitted to companionway at steps, steps fitted with brass treads.

OUTSIDE FINISH

The hull to be carefully planed and smoothed outside.

To be thoroughly caulked with cotton and seams filled with white lead putty. To have one coat priming; topsides three coats approved color white lead paint, and bottom two coats of special anti-fouling paint of approved color and brand.

Scroll work on bows and quarters, 1" groove on sheer strake, and name hail on stern to be cut and gilded with gold leaf, Spars, rails, inside of bulwarks etc., to have two coats of Kyanize No. 1 priming and two coats best spar varnish.

PLUMBING

One 200 Gal. 18 gauge galvanized iron fresh water tank located as shown. It shall have in addition two transverse and two longitudinal swash plates dividing the interior into equal portions and a flanged union for coupling on a ½" vent pipe, swash plates to have holes around the edges to insure perfect drainage from end to end, tank to have unions for connecting supply and service pipes.

Galley sink 12" x 16" enameled with drain pipe leading to 20 Gallon galvanized iron waste tank below. Galley pump Sand's Fig. S-709. Waste pump under sink Sand's Fig. S-704 piped to waste tank, discharge piped to side about 3" below L.W.L., sea connection to be a brass valve with flange to hull, bedded in white lead and securely fastened. Valve handle to be easily accessible.

Both lavatories, galley sink and ice box drain are to be piped to waste tank and fitted with traps.

Owner's toilet to be fitted with Sand's lavatory Plate S-209A complete, and guest's with Plate S-209 lavatory with a soap holder, and Plate S-701 basin pump substituted for faucets.

Lavatories to be placed at least one foot above L.W.L.

Bilge Pump:- A 3½" copper bilge pump complete with deck plate, piped to lowest part of bilge and fitted with strainer.

Ice chest to be lined throughout, including shelves, with heavy sheet zinc all joints soldered and made watertight. Waste pipe to be heavy ¾" lead pipe with trap just below ice chest, and waste from here piped to waste tank.

Sand's water closets to be fitted where indicated to have oak seat and cover, sea cocks to be fitted on all discharge and supply pipes through hull.

Bulkhead, deck and other woodwork close to stove to be covered with heavy sheet zinc worked on furring strips. Edges of zinc to be turned under, smoke pipe from galley stove to deck to be heavy galvanized sheet iron with two elbows, deck iron to be fitted in deck just forward of house. Piping to have drain cocks where necessary so that all water may be drawn from the piping in Winter.

SPAR IRON WORK

All as per plans, of best Norway iron, All lugs to be worked from solid iron, and not welded. All iron work and fastenings to be carefully galvanized, fitted to spars and efficiently secured.

STANDING RIGGING

Galvanized plow steel wire yacht rigging, arrangement and size shown; all eyes parcelled with cotton and covered with raw hide. Shrouds to be set up with lanyards and dead eyes.

RUNNING RIGGING

Plymouth Cordage Co's. best Manila, four strand, size to fit blocks. Jib sheet pennant and bridles of flexible galvanized steel wire.

BLOCKS

A complete set of Merriman Brothers blocks as per appended list, all to have ash shells. Galvanized Norway iron straps and fittings of at least equal strength to largest rope they may carry.

All parts to be finished in first class manner and woodwork shellaced and varnished. All blocks to be tagged and marked by the block maker to indicate location.

SAILS
To be supplied by owner and bent on by builder.

GROUND TACKLE
Two galvanized steel anchors, Cape Ann type, one 150 pounds, one 200 pounds.

100 fathoms 6" Manila cable for large anchor, 40 fathoms galvanized B.B.B. chain for small anchor.

OUTFIT
The owner will supply boats, lanterns, lamps, sailing and riding lights, binnacle, bell, nautical instruments, upholstery and linen, kitchen and table ware, boatswain's stores and like movable outfit, but these shall be put in place and secured by the builder. Builder shall supply yacht gangway, galvanized rail stanchions, boat boom with fittings, two sets davits with blocks, gear etc.

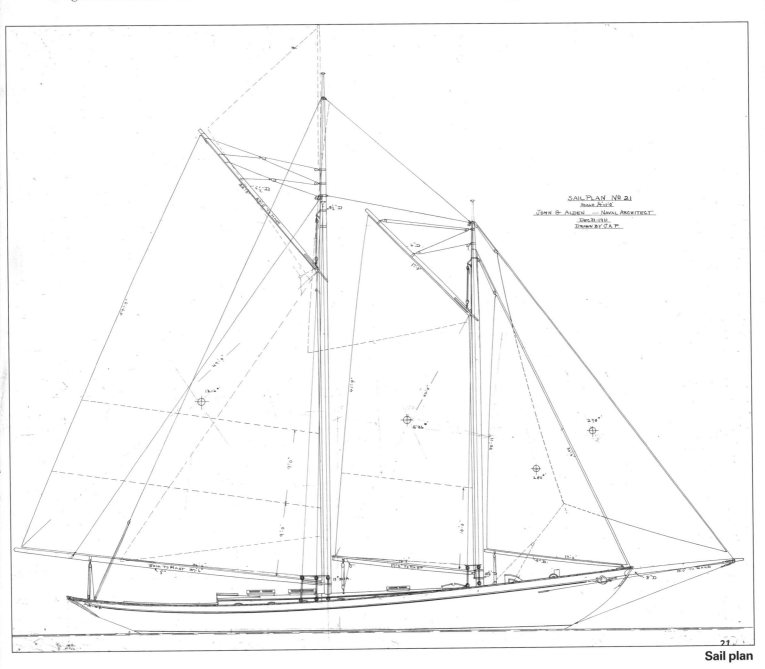

Sail plan

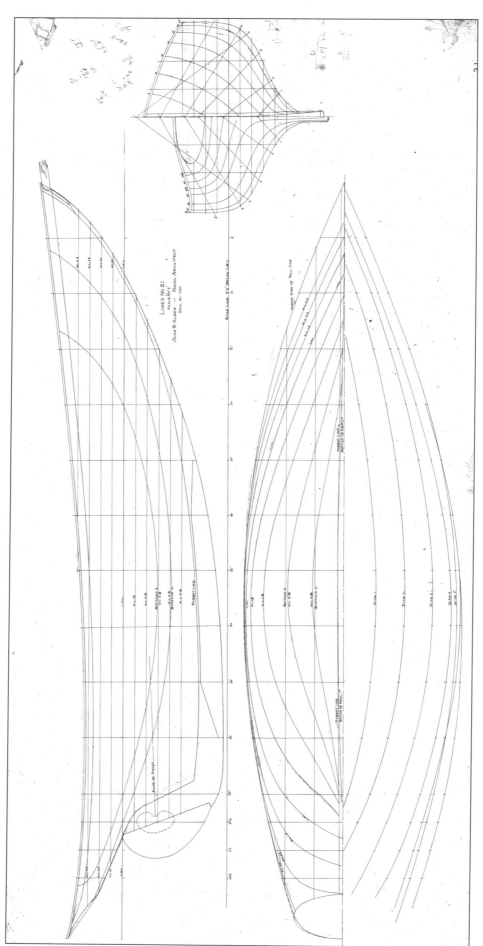

LINES No. 21
SCALE 3/8"=1'
JOHN G. ALDEN — NAVAL ARCHITECT
DEC. 31 · 1911

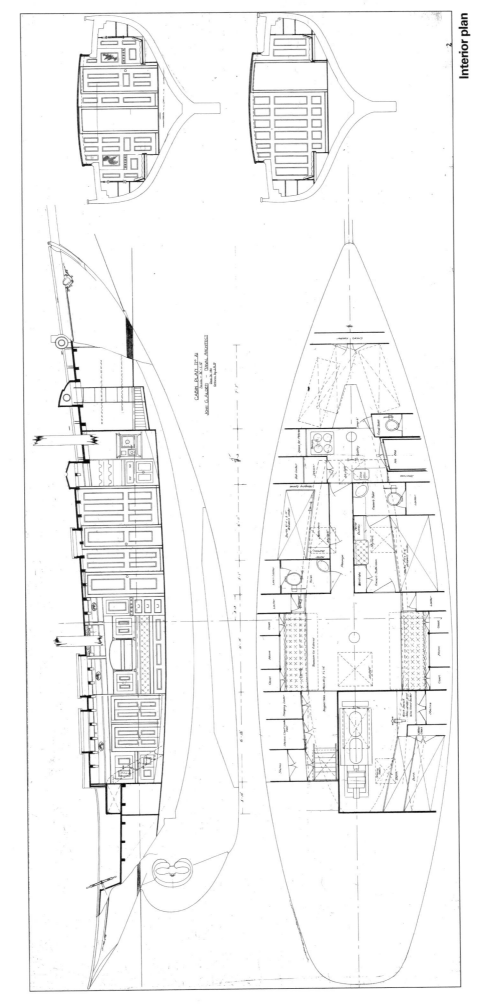

94

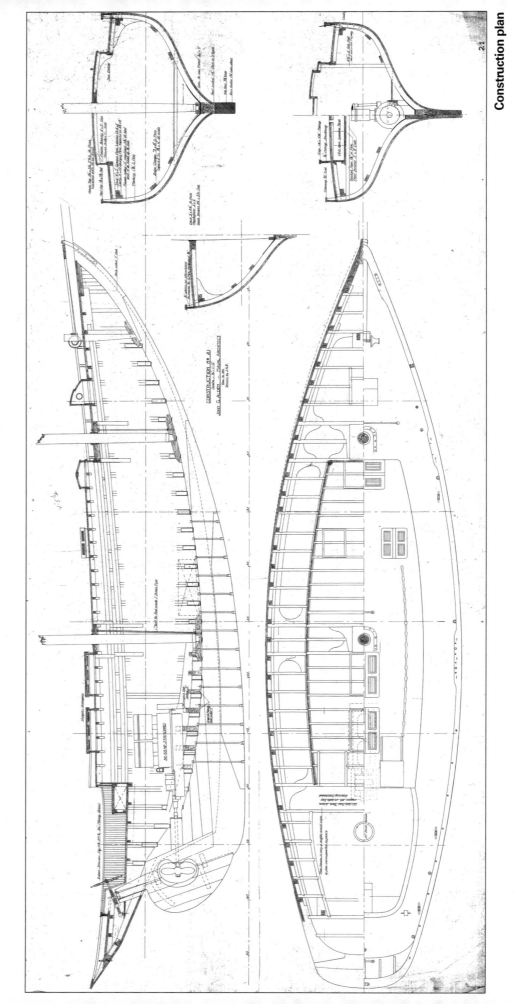